Excel® 2010

FOR

DUMMIES®

POCKET EDITION

by Greg Harvey, PhD

WILEY

John Wiley & Sons, Inc.

Excel® 2010 For Dummies®, Pocket Edition

Published by
John Wiley & Sons, Inc.
111 River Street
Hoboken, NJ 07030-5774
www.wiley.com

Copyright © 2012 by John Wiley & Sons, Inc., Hoboken, New Jersey

Published by John Wiley & Sons, Inc., Hoboken, New Jersey

Published simultaneously in Canada

For general information on our other products and services, please contact our Customer Care Department within the U.S. at 877-762-2974, outside the U.S. at 317-572-3993, or fax 317-572-4002.

For technical support, please visit www.wiley.com/techsupport.

Wiley publishes in a variety of print and electronic formats and by print-on-demand. Some material included with standard print versions of this book may not be included in e-books or in print-on-demand.

ISBN: 978-1-118-38537-1 (print); 978-1-118-43002-6 (e-pub); 978-1-118-43007-1 (e-mobi); 978-1-118-43001-9 (e-pdf)

Manufactured in the United States of America

10 9 8 7 6 5 4 3 2 1

WILEY

Publisher's Acknowledgments

We're proud of this book; please send us your comments at `http://dummies.custhelp.com`. For other comments, please contact our Customer Care Department within the U.S. at 877-762-2974, outside the U.S. at 317-572-3993, or fax 317-572-4002.

Some of the people who helped bring this book to market include the following:

Acquisitions and Editorial

Editorial Manager and Project Editor: Jodi Jensen

Sr. Acquisitions Editor: Katie Feltman

Copy Editor: Brian Walls

Technical Editors: Mike Talley, Joyce Nielsen

Editorial Assistant: Leslie Saxman

Sr. Editorial Assistant: Cherie Case

Cover Photo: © iStockphoto.com / nicolas hansen

Composition Services

Senior Project Coordinator: Kristie Rees

Layout and Graphics: Melanee Habig, Lavonne Roberts

Proofreaders: John Greenough, Toni Settle

Publishing and Editorial for Technology Dummies

Richard Swadley, Vice President and Executive Group Publisher

Andy Cummings, Vice President and Publisher

Mary Bednarek, Executive Acquisitions Director

Mary C. Corder, Editorial Director

Publishing for Consumer Dummies

Kathleen Nebenhaus, Vice President and Executive Publisher

Composition Services

Debbie Stailey, Director of Composition Services

Table of Contents

Introduction..**1**

About This Book.. 1

Conventions Used in This Book...................................... 1

Chapter 1: The Excel 2010 User Experience **3**

Excel's Ribbon User Interface.. 4

Starting Excel 23

Help Is on the Way 26

Chapter 2: Creating a Spreadsheet from Scratch.....27

So What Will You Put in That
    New Workbook of Yours?...................................... 28

Doing the Data Entry Thing....................................... 30

It Takes All Types 33

Fixing Data Entry Mistakes....................................... 46

Taking the Drudgery out of Data Entry........................ 50

Making Formulas Function Better 58

Making Sure Your Data Is Safe 67

Chapter 3: Editing a Spreadsheet **71**

Opening the Workbook for Editing 73

Much Ado about Undo 80

Doing the Old Drag-and-Drop 82

Formulas on AutoFill.. 86

Let's Be Clear about Deleting Stuff.............................. 98

Staying in Step with Insert....................................... 100

Chapter 4: Formatting a Spreadsheet.............**103**

Choosing a Group of Cells 104

Formatting from the Home Tab 112

Formatting Cells Close to the Source
    with the Mini-Toolbar... 114

Using the Format Cells Dialog Box.............................. 116

Calibrating Columns.. 125

Rambling Rows 127
Futzing with Fonts 128
Altering the Alignment 130

Chapter 5: Printing a Spreadsheet **141**

Taking a Gander at the Pages in
Page Layout View 142
Checking and Printing a Report
from the Print Panel 144
Printing the Current Worksheet 147
My Page Was Set Up! 148
From Header to Footer 158
Solving Page Break Problems 161
Letting Your Formulas All Hang Out 165

Chapter 6: Top Ten Beginner Basics **167**

Starting Excel 2010 167
Auto-Launching Excel 2010 167
Scrolling 168
Starting a New Workbook 168
Activating an Open Workbook 168
Entering Stuff into a Worksheet 169
Editing Contents of a Cell 169
Choosing Excel Commands 169
Saving Your Work 170
Exiting Excel 170

Introduction

• •

*E*xcel 2010 For Dummies, Pocket Edition, covers the fundamental techniques you need to know in order to create, edit, format, and print your own spreadsheets. This book concentrates on spreadsheets because spreadsheets are what most regular folks create with Excel.

About This Book

This book isn't meant to be read cover to cover. Although its chapters are loosely organized in a logical order, each topic covered in a chapter is really meant to stand on its own.

In Excel, as with most other sophisticated programs, you usually have more than one way to do a task. For the sake of your sanity, I have purposely limited the choices by usually giving you only the most efficient ways to do a particular task.

Conventions Used in This Book

The following information gives you the lowdown on how things look in this book.

Keyboard and mouse

Throughout the book, you'll find Ribbon command sequences separated by a command arrow, as in:

Home➪Copy

You click the Home tab on the Ribbon (if it isn't displayed already) and then click the Copy button.

If the sequence also involves selecting an item from a drop-down menu, it looks like this:

```
Formulas⇨Calculation Options⇨Manual
```

When I ask you to type something in a cell, the part you type generally appears in **bold**.

Occasionally, I give you a *hot key combination* that you can press in order to choose a command from the keyboard rather than clicking buttons on the Ribbon with the mouse. Hot key combinations are written like this: Alt+FS or Ctrl+S. You press the Alt key until the hot key letters appear in little squares all along the Ribbon. At that point, you can release the Alt key and start typing the hot key letters.

Special icons

The following icons are placed in the margins to point out stuff you may or may not want to read.

 This icon alerts you to nerdy discussions that you may well want to skip (or read when no one else is around).

 This icon alerts you to shortcuts or other valuable hints related to the topic at hand.

 This icon alerts you to information to keep in mind if you want to meet with a modicum of success.

 This icon alerts you to information to keep in mind if you want to avert complete disaster.

Chapter 1

The Excel 2010 User Experience

In This Chapter

▶ Getting familiar with the Excel 2010 program window and Backstage View

▶ Selecting commands from the Ribbon

▶ Customizing the Quick Access toolbar

▶ Surfing an Excel 2010 worksheet and workbook

▶ Methods for starting Excel 2010

▶ Getting some help with using this program

*T*he Excel 2010 user interface incorporates a single strip at the top of the worksheet called the Ribbon that puts the bulk of the Excel commands at your fingertips at all times.

Add to the Ribbon a File tab and a Quick Access toolbar — along with a few task panes (Clipboard, Clip Art, and Research) — and you end up with the handiest way yet to crunch your numbers and produce and print polished financial reports.

Best of all, this new and improved Excel user interface includes all sorts of graphical improvements. Foremost is Live Preview that shows you how your actual worksheet data would appear in a particular font, table formatting, and so on before you actually select it.

Excel's Ribbon User Interface

When you launch Excel 2010, the program opens the first of three new worksheets (named Sheet1) in a new workbook file (named Book1) inside a program window like the one shown in Figure 1-1.

Figure 1-1: The Excel 2010 program window that appears immediately after launching the program.

The Excel program window containing this worksheet of the Book1 workbook file contains these components:

- ✔ **File tab:** When clicked, this tab opens the new Backstage View — a menu on the left that contains all the document- and file-related commands, including Info (selected by default), Save, Save As, Open, Close, Recent, New, Print, and Save & Send. Additionally, there's a Help option with add-ins, an Options item that enables you to change many of Excel's default settings, and an Exit option to quit the program.

- ✔ **Quick Access toolbar:** A customizable bar containing buttons you can click to perform common tasks, such as saving your work and undoing and redoing edits.

- ✔ **Ribbon:** This bar contains the bulk of the Excel commands arranged in a series of tabs from Home through View.

- ✔ **Formula bar:** This bar displays the address of the current cell along with the contents of that cell.

- ✔ **Worksheet area:** This area contains the cells of the worksheet identified by column headings using letters along the top and row headings using numbers along the left edge; tabs for selecting new worksheets; a horizontal scroll bar to move left and right through the sheet; and a vertical scroll bar to move up and down through the sheet.

- ✔ **Status bar:** This bar keeps you informed of the program's current mode and any special keys you engage. It also enables you to select a new worksheet view and zoom in and out on the worksheet.

Going Backstage via File

To the immediate left of the Home tab on the Ribbon right below the Quick Access toolbar, you find the File tab. When you click File, the new Backstage View opens. This view contains a menu similar to the one shown in Figure 1-2. When you open the Backstage View, the Info option displays at-a-glance stats about the Excel workbook file you have open and active.

This information panel is divided into two panes. The pane on the left contains large buttons that enable you to modify the workbook's permissions, distribution, and versions. The pane on the right contains a thumbnail of the workbook followed by a list of fields detailing the workbook's various Document Properties, some of which you can change (such as Title, Tags, Categories, and Author), and many of which you can't (such as Size, Last Modified, Created, and so forth).

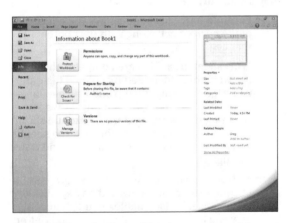

Figure 1-2: Open Backstage View for at-a-glance information about the current file, to access all file-related commands, and to modify the program options.

Above the Info option, you find the commands (Save, Save As, Open, and Close) you commonly need for working with Excel workbook files. Near the bottom, the File tab contains a Help option that, when selected, displays a Support panel in the Backstage View. This panel contains options for getting help on using Excel, customizing its default settings, as well as checking for updates to the Excel 2010 program. Below Help, you find options that you can select to change the program's settings, along with an Exit option that you can select when you're ready to close the program.

 Click the Recent option to continue editing an Excel workbook you've worked on of late. When you click the Recent option, Excel displays a panel with a list of all the workbook files recently opened in the program. To re-open a particular file for editing, all you do is click its filename in this list.

 To close the Backstage View and return to the normal worksheet view, click the File tab a second time or simply press the Escape key.

Bragging about the Ribbon

The Ribbon (shown in Figure 1-3) shows you the most commonly used options required to perform a particular Excel task.

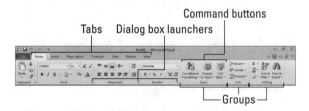

Figure 1-3: Excel's Ribbon consists of a series of tabs containing command buttons arranged into different groups.

The Ribbon contains the following components:

- ✔ **Tabs** for each of Excel's main tasks that bring together and display all the commands commonly needed to perform that core task.

- ✔ **Groups** that organize related command buttons into subtasks normally performed as part of the tab's larger core task.

- ✔ **Command buttons** within each group that you select to perform a particular action or to open a gallery from which you can click a particular thumbnail. *Note:* Some command buttons on certain tabs of the Ribbon are organized into mini-toolbars with related settings.

- ✔ **Dialog box launcher** in the lower-right corner of certain groups that opens a dialog box containing a bunch of additional options you can select.

To display more of the Worksheet area in the program window, you can minimize the Ribbon so that only its tabs display. Simply click the Minimize the Ribbon button, the first button with what looks like a greater than symbol pointing upward in the group of buttons for minimizing, maximizing, and closing the current worksheet window to the right of the Ribbon tabs and to the immediate left of the Help button. To redisplay the entire Ribbon and keep all the command buttons on its tabs displayed in the program window, click the Expand the Ribbon button.

Keeping tabs on the Excel Ribbon

The first time you launch Excel 2010, the Ribbon contains the following tabs from left to right:

- ✔ **Home** tab with the command buttons normally used when creating, formatting, and editing a spreadsheet, arranged into the Clipboard,

Font, Alignment, Number, Styles, Cells, and
Editing groups.

✔ **Insert** tab with the command buttons normally
used when adding particular elements (including
graphics, PivotTables, charts, hyperlinks, and
headers and footers) to a spreadsheet, arranged
into the Tables, Illustrations, Charts, Sparklines,
Filter, Links, Text, and Symbols groups.

✔ **Page Layout** tab with the command buttons
normally used when preparing a spreadsheet
for printing or re-ordering graphics on the
sheet, arranged into the Themes, Page Setup,
Scale to Fit, Sheet Options, and Arrange groups.

✔ **Formulas** tab with the command buttons normally used when adding formulas and functions
to a spreadsheet or checking a worksheet for
formula errors, arranged into the Function
Library, Defined Names, Formula Auditing, and
Calculation groups. *Note:* This tab also contains
a Solutions group when you activate certain
add-in programs, such as Analysis ToolPak and
Euro Currency Tools.

✔ **Data** tab with the command buttons normally
used when importing, querying, outlining, and
subtotaling the data placed into a worksheet's
data list, arranged into the Get External Data,
Connections, Sort & Filter, Data Tools, and
Outline groups. *Note:* This tab also contains an
Analysis group when you activate add-ins, such
as Analysis ToolPak and Solver.

✔ **Review** tab with the command buttons normally
used when proofing, protecting, and marking up
a spreadsheet for review by others, arranged
into the Proofing, Language, Comments, and
Changes groups. *Note:* This tab also contains an
Ink group with a sole Start Inking button when

you're running Office 2010 on a Tablet PC or a computer equipped with a digital ink tablet.

✔ **View** tab with the command buttons normally used when changing the display of the Worksheet area and the data it contains, arranged into the Workbook Views, Show, Zoom, Window, and Macros groups.

 In addition to these standard seven tabs, Excel has an eighth, optional Developer tab that you can add to the Ribbon if you do a lot of work with macros and XML files.

Although these standard tabs are the ones you always see on the Ribbon when it displays in Excel, they aren't the only things that can appear in this area. Excel can display contextual tools when you're working with a particular object that you select in the worksheet, such as a graphic image you've added or a chart or PivotTable you've created. The name of the contextual tools for the selected object appears immediately above the tab or tabs associated with the tools.

For example, Figure 1-4 shows a worksheet after you click the embedded chart to select it. As you can see, clicking the chart adds the contextual tool called Chart Tools to the very end of the Ribbon. The Chart Tools contextual tool has its own three tabs: Design (selected), Layout, and Format. Note, too, that the command buttons on the Design tab are arranged into groups Type, Data, Chart Layouts, Chart Styles, Location, and Mode.

 The moment you deselect the object (usually by clicking somewhere outside the object's boundaries), the contextual tool for that object and all its tabs immediately disappear from the Ribbon, leaving only the regular tabs — Home, Insert, Page Layout, Formulas, Data, Review, and View — displayed.

Chart Tools contextual tab

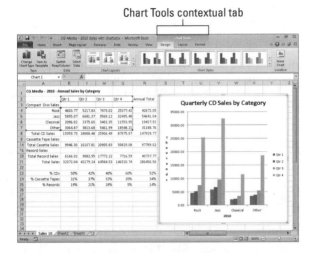

Figure 1-4: When you select certain objects in the worksheet, Excel adds contextual tools to the Ribbon with their own tabs, groups, and command buttons.

Selecting commands from the Ribbon

The most direct method for selecting commands on the Ribbon is to click the tab that contains the command button you want and then click that button in its group. For example, to insert a piece of clip art into your spreadsheet, you click the Insert tab and then click the Clip Art button to open the Clip Art task pane in the Worksheet area.

The easiest method for selecting commands on the Ribbon — if you know your keyboard well — is to press the Alt key and then type the sequence of letters designated as the hot keys for the desired tab and associated command buttons.

When you press and release the Alt key, Excel displays the hot keys for all the tabs on the Ribbon. When you type one of the Ribbon tab hot keys to select it, all the command button hot keys appear along with the hot keys for the dialog box launchers (see Figure 1-5). To select a command button or dialog box launcher, simply type its hot key letter(s).

Figure 1-5: Excel hot keys for selecting command buttons and dialog box launchers.

Customizing the Quick Access toolbar

When you start using Excel 2010, the Quick Access toolbar contains only the following few buttons:

- ✔ **Save** to save any changes made to the current workbook using the same filename, file format, and location

- ✔ **Undo** to undo the last editing, formatting, or layout change you made

- ✔ **Redo** to reapply the previous editing, formatting, or layout change that you just removed with the Undo button

The Quick Access toolbar is very customizable. It's easy to add any Excel command to this toolbar — even the obscure commands that don't rate a place on the Ribbon.

 By default, the Quick Access toolbar appears above the Ribbon tabs immediately to the right of the Excel program button (used to resize the workbook window or quit the program). To display the toolbar beneath the Ribbon immediately above the Formula bar, click the Customize Quick Access Toolbar button (the drop-down button to the right of the toolbar with a horizontal bar above a down-pointing triangle) and then click Show Below the Ribbon on its drop-down menu.

Adding command buttons to the Customize Quick Access Toolbar button's drop-down menu

When you click the Customize Quick Access Toolbar button, a drop-down menu shows you a list of commonly used commands.

When you see this list, only the Save, Undo, and Redo options are selected (indicated by the check marks); therefore, these buttons are the only buttons to appear on the Quick Access toolbar. To add any of the other commands on this menu to the toolbar, simply click the option on the drop-down menu. Excel then adds a button for that command to the end of the Quick Access toolbar.

To remove a command button that you added to the Quick Access toolbar in this manner, click the option a second time on the Customize Quick Access Toolbar button's drop-down menu. Excel removes its command button from the toolbar.

Adding Ribbon commands to the Quick Access toolbar

To add a Ribbon command to the Quick Access toolbar, simply right-click its command button on the Ribbon and then click Add to Quick Access Toolbar on its shortcut menu.

If you want to move the command button to a new location on the Quick Access toolbar or group it with other buttons on the toolbar, click the Customize Quick Access Toolbar button and then click the More Commands option near the bottom of its drop-down menu.

Excel then opens the Excel Options dialog box with the Quick Access Toolbar tab selected (similar to the one shown in Figure 1-6). On the right side of the dialog box, Excel shows all the buttons added to the Quick Access toolbar. The order in which they appear from left to right on the toolbar corresponds to the top-down order in the list box.

To reposition a particular button on the toolbar, click it in the list box on the right and then click either the Move Up button (the one with the black triangle pointing upward) or the Move Down button (the one with the black triangle pointing downward) until the button is promoted or demoted to the desired position on the toolbar.

To remove a button added from the Ribbon, right-click it on the Quick Access toolbar and then click the Remove from Quick Access Toolbar option on its shortcut menu.

Having fun with the Formula bar

The Formula bar displays the cell address (determined by a column letter(s) followed by a row number) and the contents of the current cell. For example, cell A1 is the first cell of each worksheet at the intersection of column A and row 1; cell XFD1048576 is the last cell of each worksheet at the intersection of column XFD and row 1048576. The type of entry you make determines the contents of the current cell: text or numbers, for example, if you enter a heading or particular value, or the details of a formula if you enter a calculation.

Figure 1-6: Use the Quick Access Toolbar tab of the Excel Options dialog box to customize the Quick Access toolbar.

The Formula bar has three sections:

- ✔ **Name box:** The left-most section that displays the address of the current cell address.

- ✔ **Formula bar buttons:** The second, middle section that appears as a rather nondescript button displaying only an indented circle on the left (used to narrow or widen the Name box) and the Insert Function button (labeled *fx*) on the right. When you start making or editing a cell entry, Cancel (an *X*) and Enter (a check mark) buttons appear between them.

- ✔ **Cell contents:** The third, right-most white area to the immediate right of the Insert Function button takes up the rest of the bar and expands as necessary to display really long cell entries that won't fit in the normal area.

The cell contents section of the Formula bar is important because it *always* shows you the contents of the cell even when the worksheet does not. (When you're dealing with a formula, Excel displays only the calculated result in the cell in the worksheet and not the formula by which that result is derived.) Additionally, you can edit the contents of the cell in this area at any time. Similarly, when the cell contents area is blank, you know that the cell is empty as well.

What to do in the Worksheet area

The Worksheet area is where most of the Excel spreadsheet action takes place. It's the place that displays the cells in different sections of the current worksheet, and it's where you do all your spreadsheet data entry and formatting, not to mention a great deal of your editing.

To enter or edit data in a cell, that cell must be current. Excel indicates that a cell is current in three ways:

✔ The cell cursor — the dark black border surrounding the cell's entire perimeter — appears in the cell.

✔ The address of the cell appears in the Name box of the Formula bar.

✔ The cell's column letter(s) and row number are shaded (in a kind of an orange-beige color on most monitors) in the column headings and row headings that appear at the top and left of the Worksheet area, respectively.

Moving around the worksheet

An Excel worksheet contains far too many columns and rows for all a worksheet's cells to be displayed at one time. Therefore, Excel offers many methods for moving the cell cursor around the worksheet to the cell where you want to enter new data or edit existing data:

- ✔ Click the desired cell — assuming that the cell is displayed within the section of the sheet visible in the Worksheet area.
- ✔ Click the Name box, type the address of the desired cell, and then press the Enter key.
- ✔ Press F5 to open the Go To dialog box, type the address of the desired cell into its Reference text box, and then click OK.
- ✔ Use the cursor keys, as shown in Table 1-1, to move the cell cursor to the desired cell.
- ✔ Use the horizontal and vertical scroll bars at the bottom and right edges of the Worksheet area to move the part of the worksheet that contains the desired cell and then click the cell to put the cell cursor in it.

Keystroke shortcuts for moving the cell cursor

Excel offers a wide variety of keystrokes for moving the cell cursor to a new cell. When you use one of these keystrokes, the program automatically scrolls a new part of the worksheet into view if required to move the cell pointer. In Table 1-1, I summarize these keystrokes, including how far each one moves the cell pointer from its starting position.

Table 1-1   Keystrokes for Moving the Cell Cursor

Keystroke	Where the Cell Cursor Moves
→ or Tab	Cell to the immediate right.
← or Shift+Tab	Cell to the immediate left.
↑	Cell up one row.
↓	Cell down one row.
Home	Cell in Column A of the current row.
Ctrl+Home	First cell (A1) of the worksheet.
Ctrl+End or End, Home	Cell in the worksheet at the intersection of the last column that has data in it and the last row that has data in it (that is, the last cell of the so-called active area of the worksheet).
Page Up	Cell one full screen up in the same column.
Page Down	Cell one full screen down in the same column.

Note: In the case of those keystrokes that use arrow keys, you must either use the arrows on the cursor keypad or else have the Num Lock disengaged on the numeric keypad of your keyboard.

When you use Ctrl and an arrow key to move around in a table, you hold down Ctrl while you press one of the four arrow keys (indicated by the + symbol in keystrokes, such as Ctrl+→).

When you use End and an arrow-key alternative, you must press and then release the End key *before* you press the arrow key (indicated by the comma in keystrokes, such as End, →). Pressing and releasing the End key causes the End Mode indicator to appear on the status bar. This is your sign that Excel is ready for you to press one of the four arrow keys.

 You can use the Scroll Lock key to "freeze" the position of the cell pointer in the worksheet so that you can scroll new areas of the worksheet in view with keystrokes, such as PgUp (Page Up) and PgDn (Page Down), without changing the cell pointer's original position. (In essence, making these keystrokes work in the same manner as the scroll bars.)

After engaging Scroll Lock, when you scroll the worksheet with the keyboard, Excel does not select a new cell while it brings a new section of the worksheet into view. To "unfreeze" the cell pointer when scrolling the worksheet via the keyboard, you just press the Scroll Lock key again.

Tips on using the scroll bars

To understand how scrolling works in Excel, imagine its humongous worksheet as a papyrus scroll attached to rollers on the left and right. To bring into view a section of papyrus hidden on the right, you crank the left roller until the section with the cells that you want to see appears. Likewise, to scroll into view a worksheet section hidden on the left, you crank the right roller until the section of cells appears.

You can use the horizontal scroll bar at the bottom of the Worksheet area to scroll back and forth through the columns of a worksheet and the vertical scroll bar to scroll up and down through its rows. To scroll a column or a row at a time in a particular direction, click the appropriate scroll arrow at the ends of the scroll bar. To jump immediately back to the originally displayed area of the worksheet after scrolling through single columns or rows in this fashion, simply click the area in the scroll bar that now appears in front of or after the scroll bar.

You can resize the horizontal scroll bar making it wider or narrower by dragging the button that appears to the immediate left of its left scroll arrow. Just keep in mind when working in a workbook that contains a whole bunch of worksheets that widening the horizontal scroll bar can hide the display of the workbook's later sheet tabs.

To scroll very quickly through columns or rows of the worksheet, hold down the Shift key and then drag the scroll button in the appropriate direction within the scroll bar until the columns or rows that you want to see appear on the screen in the Worksheet area. When you hold down the Shift key while you scroll, the scroll button within the scroll bar becomes skinny, and a ScreenTip appears next to the scroll bar, keeping you informed of the letter(s) of the columns or the numbers of the rows that you're whizzing through.

If your mouse has a wheel, you can use it to scroll directly through the columns and rows of the worksheet without using the horizontal or vertical scroll bars. Simply position the white cross mouse pointer in the center of the Worksheet area and then hold down the wheel button of the mouse. When the mouse pointer changes to a four-pointed arrow with a black dot in its center, drag the mouse pointer in the appropriate direction (left and right to scroll through columns or up and down to scroll through rows) until the desired column or row comes into view in the Worksheet area.

Surfing the sheets in a workbook

Each new workbook you open in Excel 2010 contains three blank worksheets, each with its own 16,384 columns and 1,048,576 rows (giving you a truly staggering 51,539,607,552 blank cells!). But, that's not all. If ever you need more worksheets in your workbook, you can add them simply by clicking the Insert Worksheet button that appears to the immediate right of the last sheet tab (see Figure 1-7) or by pressing Shift+F11.

On the left side of the bottom of the Worksheet area, the Sheet Tab scroll buttons appear followed by the actual tabs for the worksheets in your workbook and the Insert Worksheet button. To activate a worksheet for editing, you select it by clicking its sheet tab. Excel lets you know what sheet is active by displaying the sheet name in boldface type and making its tab appear on top of the others.

Don't forget the Ctrl+Page Down and Ctrl+Page Up shortcut keys for selecting the next and previous sheet, respectively, in your workbook.

First sheet
|Previous sheet
||Next sheet
|||Last sheet
||||Current sheet

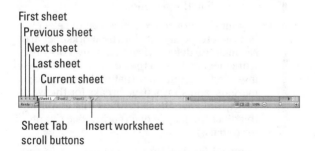

Sheet Tab   Insert worksheet
scroll buttons

Figure 1-7: The Sheet Tab scroll buttons, sheet tabs, and Insert Worksheet button enable you to activate your worksheets and add to them.

If your workbook contains too many sheets for all the tabs to display at the bottom of the Worksheet area, use the Sheet Tab scroll buttons to bring new tabs into view (so that you can then click them to activate them). You click the Next Sheet button to scroll the next hidden sheet tab into view or the Last Sheet button to scroll the last group of completely or partially hidden tabs into view.

Showing off the Status bar

The Status bar is the last component at the very bottom of the Excel program window (see Figure 1-8). The Status bar contains the following:

- ✔ **Mode indicator** that shows the current state of the Excel program (Ready, Edit, and so on) as well as any special keys that are engaged (Caps Lock, Num Lock, and Scroll Lock).

- ✔ **AutoCalculate indicator** that displays the average and sum of all the numerical entries in the current cell selection along with the count of every cell in the selection.

- ✔ **Layout selector** that enables you to select between three layouts for the Worksheet area: Normal, the default view that shows only the worksheet cells with the column and row headings; Page Layout View that adds rulers, page margins, and shows page breaks for the worksheet; and Page Break Preview that enables you to adjust the paging of a report. (See Chapter 5 for details.)

- ✔ **Zoom slider** that enables you to zoom in and out on the cells in the Worksheet area by dragging the slider to the right or left, respectively.

Layout selector

Mode indicator   Auto Calculate indicator   Zoom slider

Figure 1-8: The Status bar displays the program's current standing and enables you to select new worksheet views.

 The Num Lock indicator tells you that you can use the numbers on the numeric keypad for entering values in the worksheet. This keypad will most often be separate from the regular keyboard (on the right side if you're using a separate keyboard) and embedded in keys on the right side of the keyboard on almost all laptop computers where the keyboard is built in to the computer.

Starting Excel

Use the Start Search box at the bottom of the Windows Vista Start menu or the Search Programs and Files search box on the Windows 7 Start menu to locate Excel on your computer and launch the program:

1. **Click the Start button on the Windows taskbar to open the Windows Start menu.**

2. **Click the Start menu's search text box and type the letters** exc **to have Windows locate Microsoft Office Excel 2010 on your computer.**

3. **Click the Microsoft Excel 2010 option that now appears in the left Programs column on the Start menu.**

Alternatively, you can launch Excel from the Windows Start menu by clicking Start➪All Programs➪Microsoft Office➪Microsoft Excel 2010.

Adding a Microsoft Excel 2010 shortcut to your Windows desktop

Some people like to have the Excel program icon appear on the Windows desktop so they can launch the program from the desktop by double-clicking the program icon. To create a Microsoft Excel 2010 program shortcut for your Windows desktop, you follow these steps:

1. **Click the Windows Start button and then highlight the All Programs option on the Start menu.**

2. **Click the Microsoft Office option on the Windows Vista/Windows 7 Start menu.**

   Windows Vista and Windows 7 display a submenu listing the Office 2010 programs.

3. **Right-click Microsoft Excel 2010 on the Windows submenu to open its shortcut menu.**

4. **Highlight the Send To option on this menu and click Desktop (Create Shortcut) on the continuation shortcut menu.**

   Windows adds a Microsoft Excel 2010 shortcut icon to your Windows desktop that launches the program when you double-click it or right-click it and click the Open option.

Adding Excel to the Windows Quick Launch toolbar

If you want to be able to launch Excel 2010 by clicking a single button, drag the Excel icon for your Windows

Vista desktop shortcut to the Quick Launch toolbar to the immediate right of the Start button at the beginning of the Windows taskbar. When you position the icon on this toolbar, Windows indicates where the new Excel button will appear by drawing a black, vertical I-beam in front of or between the existing buttons on this bar. As soon as you release the mouse button, Windows adds an Excel 2010 button to the Quick Launch toolbar that enables you to launch the program by a single click of its icon.

Pinning an Excel icon to the Windows 7 taskbar

If your computer is running Windows 7, you can add a Microsoft Excel 2010 icon to the taskbar in addition to the standard Internet Explorer, Windows Explorer, and Windows Media Player buttons.

Simply drag and drop the Microsoft Excel 2010 icon you added earlier as a shortcut to the Windows desktop into its desired position on the Windows 7 taskbar. (See "Adding a Microsoft Excel 2010 shortcut to your Windows desktop" earlier in this chapter for details.)

 After pinning a Microsoft Excel 2010 icon to the Windows 7 taskbar, the button appears on the Windows taskbar each time you start your computer, and you can launch the Excel program simply by single clicking its icon.

Exiting Excel

When you're ready to call it a day and quit Excel, you have several choices for shutting down the program:

> ✔ Choose File➪Exit.
>
> ✔ Press Alt+FX or Alt+F4.
>
> ✔ Click the Close button (the X) in the upper-right corner of the Excel program window.

If you try to exit Excel after working on a workbook and you haven't saved your latest changes, the program displays an alert box querying whether you want to save your changes. To save your changes before exiting, click the Save command button. (For detailed information on saving documents, see Chapter 2.) If you've just been playing around in the worksheet and don't want to save your changes, you can abandon the document by clicking the Don't Save button.

Help Is on the Way

You can get online help with Excel 2010 anytime that you need it while using the program. Simply click the Help button (the button with the question mark icon to the immediate right of the Minimize the Ribbon button on the right side of the program window opposite the Ribbon's tabs) or press F1 to open a separate Excel Help window

When the Excel Help window opens, Excel attempts to use your Internet connection to update its topics. The opening Help window contains links that you can click to get information on what's new in the program.

Chapter 2

Creating a Spreadsheet from Scratch

- -

In This Chapter

▶ Starting a new workbook

▶ Entering the three different types of data in a worksheet

▶ Creating simple formulas by hand

▶ Fixing your data-entry boo-boos

▶ Using the AutoCorrect feature

▶ Using the AutoFill feature to complete a series of entries

▶ Entering and editing formulas containing built-in functions

▶ Totaling columns and rows of numbers with the AutoSum button

▶ Saving your precious work

- -

*I*n this chapter, you find out how to put all kinds of information into all those little, blank worksheet cells. Here you find out about the Excel AutoCorrect and AutoComplete features and how they can help cut down on errors and speed up your work. You also get some basic pointers on other smart ways to minimize the drudgery of data entry, such as filling out a series of entries with the AutoFill feature and entering the same thing in a bunch of cells all at the same time.

After discovering how to fill up a worksheet with all this raw data, you find out what has to be the most important lesson of all — how to save all that information so you don't ever have to enter the stuff again!

So What Will You Put in That New Workbook of Yours?

When you start Excel without specifying a document to open, you get a blank workbook in a new workbook window. This workbook, temporarily named Book1, contains three blank worksheets (Sheet1, Sheet2, and Sheet3). To begin to work on a new spreadsheet, you simply start entering information in the first sheet of the Book1 workbook window.

The ins and outs of data entry

Here are a few simple guidelines (a kind of data-entry etiquette, if you will) to keep in mind when you create a spreadsheet in Sheet1 of your new workbook:

✔ Whenever you can, organize your information in tables of data that use adjacent columns and rows. Start the tables in the upper-left corner of the worksheet and work your way down the sheet, rather than across the sheet. When it's practical, separate each table by no more than a single column or row.

- ✔ When you set up these tables, don't skip columns and rows just to "space out" the information. In Chapter 4, you see how to place as much white space as you want between information in adjacent columns and rows by widening columns, increasing the height in rows, and changing the alignment.

- ✔ Reserve a single column at the left edge of the table for the table's row headings.

- ✔ Reserve a single row at the top of the table for the table's column headings.

- ✔ If your table requires a title, put the title in the row above the column headings. Put the title in the same column as the row headings. Chapter 4 provides information on how to center this title across the columns of the entire table.

In Chapter 1, I make a big deal about how big each worksheet in a workbook is. You may wonder why I'm now on your case about not using that space to spread out the data that you enter into it. After all, given all the real estate that comes with each Excel worksheet, you'd think conserving space would be one of the last things you'd have to worry about.

You'd be 100-percent correct . . . except for one little, itty-bitty thing: Space conservation in the worksheet equals memory conservation. As a table of data grows and expands into columns and rows in new areas of the worksheet, Excel decides that it had better reserve a certain amount of computer memory and hold it open just in case you go crazy and fill that area with cell entries. Therefore, if you skip columns and rows that you really don't need to skip (just to cut down on all that cluttered data), you end up wasting computer memory that could store more information in the worksheet.

It's all about memory

Now you know: The amount of computer memory available to Excel determines the ultimate size of the spreadsheet you can build, not the total number of cells in the worksheets of your workbook. When you run out of memory, you've effectively run out of space — no matter how many columns and rows are still available. To maximize the information you can get into a single worksheet, always adopt the "covered wagon" approach to worksheet design by keeping your data close together.

Doing the Data Entry Thing

Before you can position the cell pointer in the cell where you want the entry, Excel must be in Ready mode (look for Ready as the Program indicator at the beginning of the Status bar). When you start typing the entry, however, Excel goes through a mode change from Ready to Enter mode (and *Enter* replaces *Ready* as the Program indicator).

If you're not in Ready mode, try pressing Esc.

As soon as you begin typing in Enter mode, the characters you type in a cell in the worksheet area simultaneously appear on the Formula bar near the top of the screen. Typing something in the current cell also triggers a change to the Formula bar because two new buttons, Cancel and Enter, appear between the Name box drop-down button and the Insert Function button.

As you continue typing, Excel displays your progress on the Formula bar and in the active cell in the worksheet (see Figure 2-1). However, the insertion point (the flashing vertical bar that acts as your cursor) displays only at the end of the characters displayed in the cell.

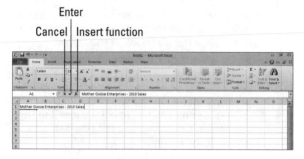

Figure 2-1: What you type appears both in the current cell and on the Formula bar.

After you finish typing your cell entry, you still have to get it into the cell so that it stays put. To complete your cell entry and, at the same time, get Excel out of Enter mode and back into Ready mode, you can click the Enter button on the Formula bar, press the Enter key, or press one of the arrow keys ($\downarrow$, $\uparrow$, $\rightarrow$, or $\leftarrow$) to move to another cell. You can also press the Tab key or Shift+Tab keys to complete a cell entry.

Now, even though each of these alternatives gets your text into the cell, each does something a little different afterward, so please take note:

✔ If you click the Enter button (the one with the check mark) on the Formula bar, the text goes into the cell, and the cell pointer just stays in the cell containing the brand-new entry.

✔ If you press the Enter key on your keyboard, the text goes into the cell, and the cell pointer moves down to the cell below in the next row.

✔ If you press one of the arrow keys, the text goes into the cell, and the cell pointer moves to the next cell in the direction of the arrow.

✔ If you press Tab, the text goes into the cell, and the cell pointer moves to the adjacent cell in the column on the immediate right (the same as pressing the → key). If you press Shift+Tab, the cell pointer moves to the adjacent cell in the column on the immediate left (the same as pressing the ← key).

No matter which method you choose, as soon as you complete your entry in the current cell, Excel deactivates the Formula bar by removing the Cancel and Enter buttons. Thereafter, the data you entered continues to appear in the cell in the worksheet (with certain exceptions that I discuss later in this chapter), and every time you put the cell pointer into that cell, the data reappears on the Formula bar as well.

If, while still typing an entry or after finishing typing but prior to completing the entry, you realize that you're just about to stick it in the wrong cell, you can clear and deactivate the Formula bar by clicking the Cancel button (the one with the X in it) or by pressing Esc. If, however, you don't realize that you had the wrong cell until after you enter your data there, you have to either move the entry to the correct cell (something you find out how to do in Chapter 3) or delete the entry and re-enter the data in the correct cell.

It Takes All Types

Excel constantly analyzes the stuff you type and classifies it into one of three possible data types: a piece of *text*, a *value*, or a *formula*. If Excel finds that the entry is a formula, the program automatically calculates the formula and displays the computed result in the worksheet cell (you continue to see the formula itself, however, on the Formula bar). If Excel is satisfied that the entry does not qualify as a formula, the program then determines whether the entry should be classified as text or as a value.

Excel makes this distinction between text and values so that it knows how to align the entry in the worksheet. It aligns text entries with the left edge of the cell and values with the right edge. Because most formulas work properly only when they are fed values, by differentiating text from values, the program knows which will and will not work in the formulas that you build. Suffice to say that you can foul up your formulas but good if they refer to any cells containing text where Excel expects values to be.

The telltale signs of text

A text entry is simply an entry that Excel can't pigeonhole as either a formula or value. Consequently, text is the catch-all category of Excel data types. As a practical rule, most text entries (also known as *labels*) are a combination of letters and punctuation or letters and numbers. Text is used mostly for titles, headings, and notes in the worksheet.

You can tell right away whether Excel has accepted a cell entry as text because text entries automatically align at the left edge of the cell. If the text entry is wider than the cell can display, the data spills into the neighboring cell or cells on the right, *as long as those cells remain blank* (see Figure 2-2).

If, sometime later, you enter information in a cell that contains spillover text from a cell to its left, Excel cuts off the spillover of the long text entry (see Figure 2-3). Not to worry: Excel doesn't actually lop these characters off the cell entry — it simply shaves the display to make room for the new entry. To redisplay the seemingly missing portion of the long text entry, you have to widen the column that contains the cell where the text is entered. (To find out how to do this, see Chapter 4.)

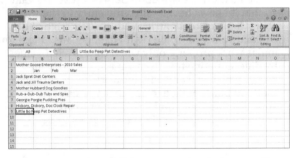

Figure 2-2: Long text entries spill over into neighboring blank cells.

How Excel evaluates its values

Values are the building blocks of most of the formulas that you create in Excel. As such, values come in two flavors: numbers that represent quantities (*14* stores or *$140,000* dollars) and numbers that represent dates *(July 30, 1995)* or times (*2* p.m.).

	A3		▾	fx	Jack Sprat Diet Centers				

◢	A	B	C	D	E	F	G	H	I
1	Mother Goose Enterprises - 2010 Sales								
2		Jan	Feb	Mar					
3	Jack Sprat	80138.58							
4	Jack and Jill Trauma Centers								
5	Mother Hubbard Dog Goodies								
6	Rub-a-Dub-Dub Tubs and Spas								
7	Georgie Porgie Pudding Pies								
8	Hickory, Dickory, Doc Clock Repair								
9	Little Bo Peep Pet Detectives								
10									
11									
12									
13									
14									
15									

Figure 2-3: Entries in cells to the right cut off the spillover text in cells on the left.

You can tell whether Excel has accepted your entry as a value because values automatically align at the right edge of their cells. If the value that you enter is wider than the column containing the cell can display, Excel automatically converts the value to (of all things) *scientific notation.* To restore a value that's been converted into that weird scientific notation stuff to a regular number, simply widen the column for that cell. (Read how in Chapter 4.)

Making sure Excel's got your number

When building a new worksheet, you'll probably spend a lot of your time entering numbers, representing all types of quantities from money that you made (or lost) to the percentage of the office budget that went to coffee and donuts.

To enter a numeric value that represents a positive quantity, like the amount of money you made last year, just select a cell, type the numbers — for example, **459600** — and complete the entry in the cell by clicking the Enter button, pressing the Enter key, and so on. To enter a numeric value that represents a negative quantity, such as the amount of money the office spent on coffee and donuts last year, begin the entry with the minus sign or hyphen (–) before typing the numbers and then complete the entry. For example, **–175**.

If you're trained in accounting, you can enclose the negative number (that's *expense* to you) in parenthe-ses. You'd enter it like this: **(175)**. If you go to all the trouble to use parentheses for your negatives (expenses), Excel goes ahead and automatically con-verts the number so that it begins with a minus sign; if you enter **(175)** in the Coffee and Donut expense cell, Excel spits back -175. (Relax, you can find out how to get your beloved parentheses back for the expenses in your spreadsheet in Chapter 4.)

With numeric values that represent dollar amounts, like the amount of money you made last year, you can include dollar signs ($) and commas (,) just as they appear in the printed or handwritten numbers you're working from. Just be aware that when you enter a number with commas, Excel assigns a number format to the value that matches your use of commas. (For more information on number formats and how they are used, see Chapter 4.) Likewise, when you preface a financial figure with a dollar sign, Excel assigns an appropriate dollar-number format to the value (one that automatically inserts commas between the thousands).

When entering numeric values with decimal places, use the period as the decimal point. When you enter decimal values, the program automatically adds a zero before the decimal point (Excel inserts 0.34 in a cell when you enter **.34**) and drops trailing zeros entered after the decimal point (Excel inserts 12.5 in a cell when you enter **12.50**).

If you don't know the decimal equivalent for a value that contains a fraction, you can just go ahead and enter the value with its fraction. For example, if you don't know that 2.1875 is the decimal equivalent for 2³⁄₁₆, just type **2 ³⁄₁₆** (making sure to add a space between the 2 and 3) in the cell. After completing the entry, when you put the cell pointer in that cell, you see $2^3/_{16}$ in the cell of the worksheet, but 2.1875 appears on the Formula bar.

If you need to enter simple fractions, such as ¾ or ⅝, you must enter them as a mixed number preceded by zero; for example, enter **0 ¾** or **0 ⅝** (be sure to include a space between the zero and the fraction). Otherwise, Excel thinks that you're entering the dates March 4 (¾) and May 8 (⅝).

When entering in a cell a numeric value that represents a percentage (so much out of a hundred), you have this choice:

- ✔ You can either divide the number by 100 and enter the decimal equivalent (by moving the decimal point two places to the left like your teacher taught you; for example, enter **.12** for 12 percent).

- ✔ You can enter the number with the percent sign (for example, enter **12%**).

Either way, Excel stores the decimal value in the cell (0.12 in this example). If you use the percent sign, Excel assigns a percentage-number format to the value in the worksheet so that it appears as 12%.

Entering dates with no debate

At first look, it may strike you as a bit odd to enter dates and times as values in the cells of a worksheet rather than text. The reason for this is simple, really: Dates and times entered as values can be used in formula calculations, whereas dates and times entered as text cannot. For example, if you enter two dates as values, you can then set up a formula that subtracts the more recent date from the older date and returns the number of days between them. This kind of thing just couldn't happen if you were to enter the two dates as text entries.

Excel determines whether the date or time that you type is a value or text by the format that you follow. If you follow one of Excel's built-in date and time formats, the program recognizes the date or time as a value. If you don't follow one of the built-in formats, the program enters the date or time as a text entry — it's as simple as that.

Excel recognizes the following time formats:

3 AM or 3 PM

3 A or 3 P (upper- or lowercase a or p — Excel inserts 3:00 AM or 3:00 PM)

3:21 AM or 3:21 PM (upper- or lowercase am or pm)

3:21:04 AM or 3:21:04 PM (upper- or lowercase am or pm)

15:21

15:21:04

Excel isn't fussy, so you can enter the AM or PM designation in the date in any manner — uppercase letters, lowercase letters, or even a mix of the two.

Excel knows the following date formats. (Month abbreviations always use the first three letters of the name of the month: Jan, Feb, Mar, and so forth.)

November 6, 2008 or November 6, 08 (appear in cell as 6-Nov-08)

11/6/08 or 11-6-08 (appear in cell as 11/6/2008)

6-Nov-08 or 6/Nov/08 or even 6Nov08 (all appear in cell as 6-Nov-08)

11/6 or 6-Nov or 6/Nov or 6Nov (all appear in cell as 6-Nov)

Nov-06 or Nov/06 or Nov06 (all appear in cell as 6-Nov)

Make it a date in the 21st Century

Contrary to what you may think, when entering dates in the 21st Century, you need to enter only the last two digits of the year. For example, to enter the date January 6, 2008, in a worksheet, I enter **1/6/08** in the target cell. Likewise, to put the date February 15, 2010, in a worksheet, I enter **2/15/10** in the target cell.

This system of having to put in only the last two digits of dates in the 21st Century works only for dates in the first three decades of the new century (2000 through 2029). To enter dates for the years 2030 on, you need to input all four digits of the year.

This also means, however, that to put in dates in the first three decades of the 20th Century (1900 through 1929), you must enter all four digits of the year. For example, to put in the date July 21, 1925, you have to enter **7/21/1925** in the target cell. Otherwise, if you enter just the last two digits (**25**) for the year part of the date, Excel enters a date for the year 2025 and not 1925!

Excel 2010 always displays all four digits of the year in the cell and on the Formula bar even when you only enter the last two. For example, if you enter

11/06/08 in a cell, Excel automatically displays 11/6/2008 in the worksheet cell (and on the Formula bar when that cell is current).

Therefore, by looking at the Formula bar, you can always tell when you've entered a 20th rather than a 21st Century date in a cell even if you can't keep straight the rules for when to enter just the last two digits rather than all four.

Fabricating those fabulous formulas!

As entries go in Excel, formulas are the real work-horses of the worksheet. If you set up a formula properly, it computes the correct answer when you enter the formula into a cell. From then on, the formula stays up to date, recalculating the results whenever you change any of the values that the formula uses.

You let Excel know that you're about to enter a formula (rather than some text or a value), in the current cell by starting the formula with the equal sign (=). Most simple formulas follow the equal sign with a built-in function, such as SUM or AVERAGE. (See the section "Inserting a function into a formula," later in this chapter, for more information on using functions in formulas.) Other simple formulas use a series of values or cell references that contain values separated by one or more of the following mathematical operators:

+ (plus sign) for addition

– (minus sign or hyphen) for subtraction

* (asterisk) for multiplication

/ (slash) for division

^ (caret) for raising a number to an exponential power

For example, to create a formula in cell C2 that multiplies a value entered in cell A2 by a value in cell B2, enter the following formula in cell C2: **=A2*B2**.

To enter this formula in cell C2, follow these steps:

1. **Select cell C2.**
2. **Type the entire formula** =A2*B2 **in the cell.**
3. **Press Enter.**

Or

1. **Select cell C2.**
2. **Type** = **(equal sign).**
3. **Select cell A2 in the worksheet by using the mouse or the keyboard.**

   This action places the cell reference A2 in the formula in the cell (as shown in Figure 2-4).

4. **Type * (Shift+8 on the top row of the keyboard).**

   The asterisk is used for multiplication rather than the × symbol you used in school.

5. **Select cell B2 in the worksheet by using the mouse or the keyboard.**

   This action places the cell reference B2 in the formula (as shown in Figure 2-5).

6. **Click the Enter button to complete the formula entry while keeping the cell pointer in cell C2.**

   Excel displays the calculated answer in cell C2 and the formula =A2*B2 in the Formula bar (as shown in Figure 2-6).

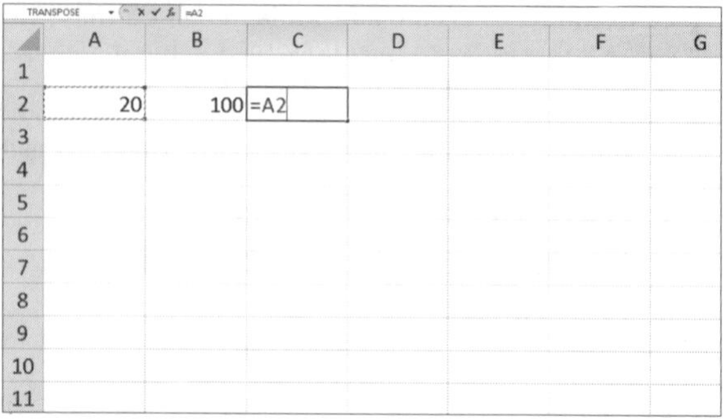

Figure 2-4: To start the formula, type = and then select cell A2.

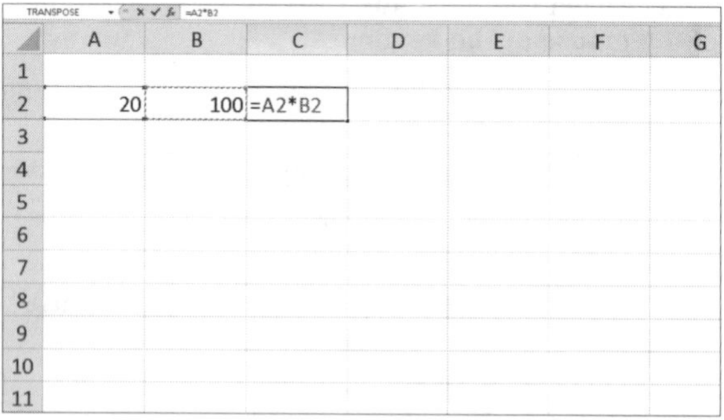

Figure 2-5: To complete the second part of the formula, type *
and select cell B2.

Excel displays the calculated result, depending on the
values currently entered in cells A2 and B2. The major
strength of the electronic spreadsheet is the capabil-
ity of formulas to change their calculated results automatically to match changes in the cells referenced by
the formulas.

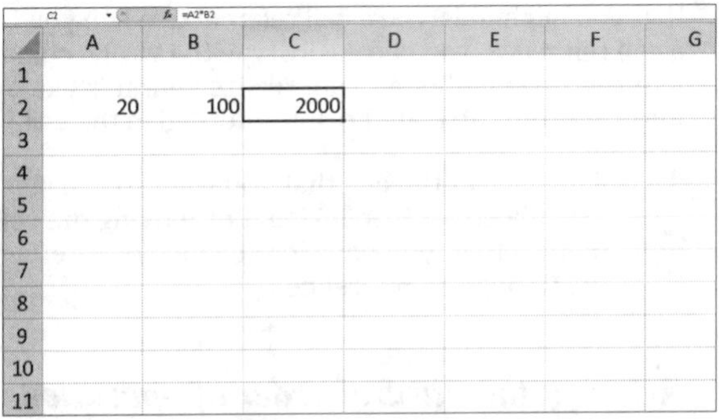

Figure 2-6: Click the Enter button, and Excel displays the answer in cell C2 while the formula appears in the Formula bar above.

Now comes the fun part: After creating a formula like the preceding one that refers to the values in certain cells (rather than containing those values itself), you can change the values in those cells, and Excel automatically recalculates the formula, using these new values and displaying the updated answer in the worksheet! Using the example shown in Figure 2-6, suppose that you change the value in cell B2 from 100 to 50. The moment that you complete this change in cell B2, Excel recalculates the formula and displays the new answer, 1000, in cell C2.

When you finish entering the formula =**A2*B2** in cell C2 of the worksheet,

If you want it, just point it out

The method of selecting the cells you use in a formula, rather than typing their cell references, is *pointing*. Pointing is quicker than typing and reduces the risk that you might mistype a cell reference. When you type a cell reference, you can easily type the wrong column letter or row number and not realize your mistake by looking at the calculated result returned in the cell.

If you select the cell that you want to use in a formula either by clicking it or moving the cell pointer to it, you have less chance of entering the wrong cell reference.

Altering the natural order of operations

Many formulas that you create perform more than one mathematical operation. Excel performs each operation, moving from left to right, according to a strict pecking order (the natural order of arithmetic operations). In this order, multiplication and division pull more weight than addition and subtraction and, therefore, perform first, even if these operations don't come first in the formula (when reading from left to right).

Consider the series of operations in the following formula:

=A2+B2*C2

If cell A2 contains the number 5, B2 contains the number 10, and C2 contains the number 2, Excel evaluates the following formula:

=5+10*2

In this formula, Excel multiplies 10 times 2 to equal 20 and then adds this result to 5 to produce the result 25.

If you want Excel to perform the addition between the values in cells A2 and B2 before the program multiplies the result by the value in cell C2, enclose the addition operation in parentheses as follows:

`= (A2+B2) *C2`

The parentheses around the addition tell Excel that you want this operation performed before the multiplication. If cell A2 contains the number 5, B2 contains the number 10, and C2 contains the number 2, Excel adds 5 and 10 to equal 15 and then multiplies this result by 2 to produce the result 30.

In fancier formulas, you may need to add more than one set of parentheses, one within another (like the wooden Russian dolls that nest within each other) to indicate the order in which you want the calculations to take place. When nesting parentheses, Excel first performs the calculation contained in the most inside pair of parentheses and then uses that result in further calculations as the program works its way outward. For example, consider the following formula:

`= (A4+ (B4-C4) ) *D4`

Excel first subtracts the value in cell C4 from the value in cell B4, adds the difference to the value in cell A4, and then finally multiplies that sum by the value in D4.

Without the additions of the two sets of nested parentheses, left to its own devices, Excel would first multiply the value in cell C4 by that in D4, add the value in A4 to that in B4, and then perform the subtraction.

Don't worry too much when nesting parentheses in a formula if you don't pair them properly so that you have a right parenthesis for every left parenthesis in the formula. If you do not include a right parenthesis for every left one, Excel displays an alert dialog box that suggests the correction needed to balance the pairs. If you agree with the program's suggested correction, you simply click the Yes button. However, be sure that you only use parentheses: ( ). Excel balks at the use of brackets — [ ] — or braces — { } — in a formula by giving you an Error alert box.

Fixing Data Entry Mistakes

When entering vast quantities of data, it's easy for those nasty little typos to creep into your work. In your pursuit of the perfect spreadsheet, here are things you can do. First, get Excel to correct certain data entry typos automatically when they happen with its AutoCorrect feature. Second, manually correct any disgusting little errors that get through, either while you're still in the process of making the entry in the cell or after the entry has gone in.

You really AutoCorrect that for me

The AutoCorrect feature is a godsend for those of us who tend to make the same stupid typos over and over. With AutoCorrect, you can alert Excel 2010 to your own particular typing gaffes and tell the program how it should automatically fix them for you.

When you first install Excel, the AutoCorrect feature already knows to automatically correct two initial capital letters in an entry (by lowercasing the second capital letter), to capitalize the name of the days of the week, and to replace a set number of text entries and typos with particular substitute text.

You can add to the list of text replacements at any time when using Excel. These text replacements can be of two types: typos that you routinely make along with the correct spelling, and abbreviations or acronyms that you type all the time along with their full forms.

To add to the replacements:

1. **Choose File⇨Options⇨Proofing or press Alt+FIP and then click the AutoCorrect Options button or press Alt+A.**

   Excel opens the AutoCorrect dialog box shown in Figure 2-7.

2. **On the AutoCorrect tab in this dialog box, enter the typo or abbreviation in the Replace text box.**

3. **Enter the correction or full form in the With text box.**

4. **Click the Add button or press Enter to add the new typo or abbreviation to the AutoCorrect list.**

5. **Click the OK button to close the AutoCorrect dialog box.**

Figure 2-7: Use the Replace and With options in the AutoCorrect dialog box to add all typos and abbreviations you want Excel to automatically correct or fill out.

Cell editing etiquette

Despite the help of AutoCorrect, some mistakes are bound to get you. How you correct them really depends upon whether you notice before or after completing the cell entry.

✔ If you catch the mistake before you complete an entry, you can delete it by pressing your Backspace key until you remove all the incorrect characters from the cell. Then you can retype the rest of the entry or the formula before you complete the entry in the cell.

✔ If you don't discover the mistake until after you've completed the cell entry, you have a choice of replacing the whole thing or editing just the mistakes.

✔ When dealing with short entries, you'll probably want to take the replacement route. To replace a cell entry, position the cell pointer in that cell, type your replacement entry, and then click the Enter button or press one of the arrow keys.

✔ When the error in an entry is relatively easy to fix and the entry is on the long side, you'll probably want to edit the cell entry rather than replace it. To edit the entry in the cell, simply double-click the cell or select the cell and then press F2.

✔ Doing either one reactivates the Formula bar by displaying the Enter and Cancel buttons once again and placing the insertion point in the cell entry in the worksheet. (If you double-click, the insertion point positions itself wherever you click; press F2, and the insertion point positions itself after the last character in the entry.)

✔ Notice also that the mode indicator changes to Edit. While in this mode, you can use the mouse or the arrow keys to position the insertion point at the place in the cell entry that needs fixing.

In Table 2-1, I list the keystrokes you can use to reposition the insertion point in the cell entry and delete unwanted characters. If you want to insert new characters at the insertion point, simply start typing. If you want to delete existing characters at the insertion point while you type new ones, press the Insert key on your keyboard to switch from the normal insert mode to overtype mode. To return to normal insert mode, press Insert a second time. When you finish making corrections to the cell entry, you must complete the edits by pressing Enter before Excel updates the contents of the cell.

 While Excel is in Edit mode, you must re-enter the edited cell contents by either clicking the Enter button or pressing Enter. You can use the arrow keys as a way to complete an entry only when the program is in Enter mode. When the program is in Edit mode, the arrow keys move the insertion point only through the entry that you're editing, not to a new cell.

Table 2-1   Keystrokes for Fixing Cell Entry Mistakes

Keystroke	What the Keystroke Does
Delete	Deletes the character to the right of the insertion point
Backspace	Deletes the character to the left of the insertion point
→	Positions the insertion point one character to the right
←	Positions the insertion point one character to the left

continued

Table 2-1 *(continued)*

Keystroke	What the Keystroke Does
↑	Positions the insertion point, when it is at the end of the cell entry, to its preceding position to the left
End or ↓	Moves the insertion point after the last character in the cell entry
Home	Moves the insertion point in front of the first character of the cell entry
Ctrl+→	Positions the insertion point in front of the next word in the cell entry
Ctrl+←	Positions the insertion point in front of the preceding word in the cell entry
Insert	Switches between insert and overtype mode

Taking the Drudgery out of Data Entry

Before leaving the topic of data entry, I feel duty-bound to cover some of the shortcuts that really help to cut down on the drudgery of this task. These data-entry tips include AutoComplete and AutoFill features as well as doing data entry in a preselected block of cells and making the same entry in a bunch of cells all at the same time.

I'm just not complete without you

AutoComplete is like a moronic mind reader who anticipates what you might want to enter next based on what you just entered. This feature comes into play only when you're entering a column of text entries. (It does not come into play when entering values or formulas or when entering a row of text entries.) When entering a column of text entries, AutoComplete looks at the kinds of entries that you make in that column and automatically duplicates them in subsequent rows whenever you start a new entry that begins with the same letter as an existing entry.

For example, suppose that I enter **Jack Sprat Diet Centers** (one of the companies owned and operated by Mother Goose Enterprises) in cell A2 and then move the cell pointer down to cell A3 in the row below and press **J** (lowercase or uppercase, it doesn't matter). AutoComplete immediately inserts the remainder of the familiar entry — *ack Sprat Diet Centers* — in this cell after the J, as shown in Figure 2-8.

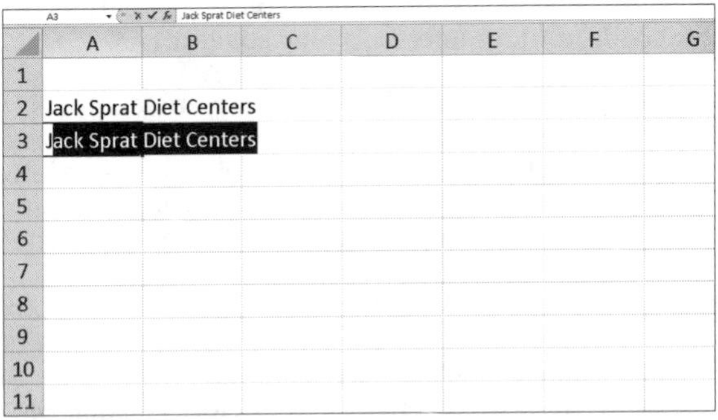

Figure 2-8: AutoComplete duplicates a previous entry if you start a new entry in the same column that begins with the same letter.

Now this is great if I happen to need Jack Sprat Diet Centers as the row heading in both cells A2 and A3. Anticipating that I might be typing a different entry that just happens to start with the same letter as the one above, AutoComplete automatically selects everything after the first letter in the duplicated entry it inserted (from *ack* on, in this example). This enables me to replace the duplicate text supplied by AutoComplete just by continuing to type. For example, after capturing the Excel screen that you see in Figure 2-8, I entered Jack and Jill Trauma Centers in cell A3.

If you override a duplicate supplied by AutoComplete in a column by typing one of your own (as in my example with changing Jack Sprat Diet Centers to Jack and Jill Trauma Centers in cell A3), you effectively shut down its ability to supply any more duplicates for that particular letter. For instance, in my example, after changing Jack Sprat Diet Centers to Jack and Jill Trauma Centers in cell A3, AutoComplete doesn't do anything if I then type **J** in cell A4. In other words, you're on your own if you don't continue to accept AutoComplete's typing suggestions.

If you find that the AutoComplete feature is really making it hard for you to enter a series of cell entries that all start with the same letter but are otherwise not alike, you can turn off the AutoComplete feature. Click File⇨Options⇨ Advanced or press Alt+FIA to select the Advanced tab of the Excel Options dialog box. Then, select the Enable AutoComplete for Cell Values check box in the Editing Options section to remove its check mark before clicking OK.

Fill 'er up with AutoFill

Many of the worksheets that you create with Excel require the entry of a series of sequential dates or numbers. For example, a worksheet may require you to title the columns with the 12 months, from

January through December, or to number the rows from 1 to 100.

Excel's AutoFill feature makes short work of this kind of repetitive task. All you have to enter is the starting value for the series. In most cases, AutoFill is smart enough to figure out how to fill out the series for you when you drag the fill handle to the right (to take the series across columns to the right) or down (to extend the series to the rows below).

 The AutoFill handle looks like this — + — and appears only when you position the mouse pointer on the lower-right corner of the active cell (or the last cell, when you've selected a block of cells). If you drag a cell selection with the white cross mouse pointer rather than the AutoFill handle, Excel simply extends the cell selection to those cells you drag through (see Chapter 4). If you drag a cell selection with the arrowhead pointer, Excel moves the cell selection (see Chapter 3).

When creating a series with the fill handle, you can drag in only one direction at a time. For example, you can fill the series or copy the entry to the range to the left or right of the cell that contains the initial values, or you can fill the series or copy to the range above or below the cell containing the initial values. You can't, however, fill or copy the series to two directions at the same time (such as down and to the right by dragging the fill handle diagonally).

While you drag the mouse, the program keeps you informed of whatever entry will be entered into the last cell selected in the range by displaying that entry next to the mouse pointer (a kind of AutoFill tips, if you will). When you release the mouse button after extending the range with the fill handle, Excel either creates a series in all the cells you select or copies

the entire range with the initial value. To the right of
the last entry in the filled or copied series, Excel also
displays a drop-down button that contains a shortcut
menu of options. You can use this shortcut menu to
override Excel's default filling or copying. For example, when you use the fill handle, Excel copies an initial value into a range of cells. But, if you want a
sequential series, you could do this by selecting the
Fill Series command on the AutoFill Options shortcut
menu.

In Figures 2-9 and 2-10, I illustrate how to use AutoFill
to enter a row of months, starting with January in cell
B2 and ending with June in cell G2. To do this, you
simply enter **January** in cell B2 and then position the
mouse pointer on the fill handle in the lower-right
corner of this cell before you drag through to cell G2
on the right (as shown in Figure 2-9). When you
release the mouse button, Excel fills in the names of
the rest of the months (February through June) in the
selected cells (as shown in Figure 2-10). Excel keeps
the cells with the series of months selected, giving
you another chance to modify the series. (If you went
too far, you can drag the fill handle to the left to cut
back on the list of months; if you didn't go far enough,
you can drag it to the right to extend the list of
months further.)

You can use the options on the AutoFill Options drop-
down menu (opened by clicking the drop-down
button that appears on the fill handle to the right of
June) to override the series created by default. To
have Excel copy January into each of the selected
cells, choose Copy Cells on this menu. To have the
program fill the selected cells with the formatting
used in cell B2 (in this case, the cell has had bold
applied to it — see Chapter 4 for details on formatting
cells), you select Fill Formatting Only on this menu.

To have Excel fill in the series of months in the selected cells without copying the formatting used in cell B2, you select the Fill without Formatting command from this shortcut menu.

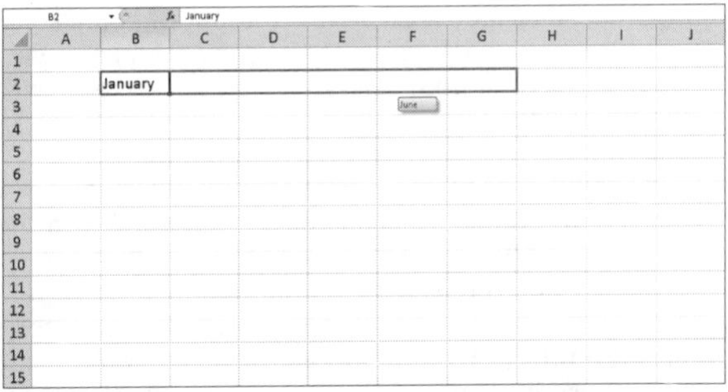

Figure 2-9: To enter a series of months, enter the first month and then drag the Fill handle in a direction to add sequential months.

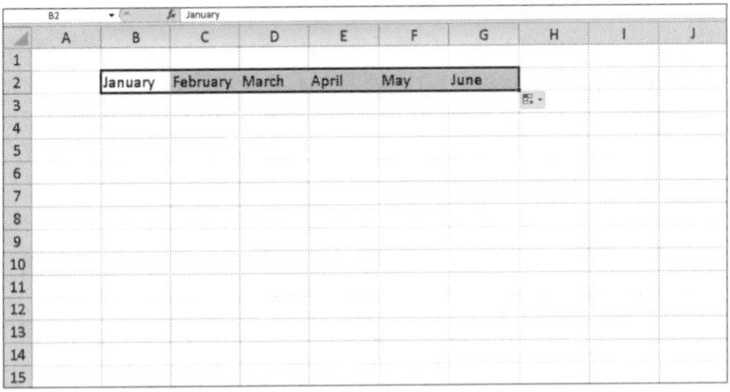

Figure 2-10: Release the mouse button, and Excel fills the cell selection with the missing months.

Working with a spaced series

AutoFill uses the initial value that you select (date, time, day, year, and so on) to design the series. You can tell AutoFill to create a series that changes by some other value: Enter two sample values in neighboring cells that describe the amount of change you want between each value in the series. Make these two values the initial selection that you extend with the fill handle.

For example, to start a series with Saturday and enter every other day across a row, enter **Saturday** in the first cell and **Monday** in the cell next door. After selecting both cells, drag the fill handle across the cells to the right as far as you need to fill out a series based on these two initial values. When you release the mouse button, Excel follows the example set in the first two cells by entering every other day (Wednesday to the right of Monday, Friday to the right of Wednesday, and so on).

Copying with AutoFill

You can use AutoFill to copy a text entry throughout a cell range (rather than fill in a series of related entries). To copy a text entry to a cell range, hold down the Ctrl key while you click and drag the Fill handle. A plus sign appears to the right of the Fill handle, which is your sign that AutoFill will *copy* the entry in the active cell instead of creating a series using it. You can also tell because the entry that appears as the AutoFill tip next to the mouse pointer while you drag contains the same text as the original cell. If you decide after copying an initial label or value to a range that you should have used it to fill in a series, click the drop-down button that appears on the fill handle at the cell with the last copied entry and then select the Fill Series command on the AutoFill Options shortcut menu that appears.

Although holding down Ctrl while you drag the fill handle copies a text entry, just the opposite is true when it comes to values! Suppose that you enter the number **17** in a cell and then drag the fill handle across the row — Excel just copies the number 17 in all the cells that you select. If, however, you hold down Ctrl while you drag the fill handle, Excel then fills out the series (17, 18, 19, and so on). If you forget and create a series of numbers when you only need the value copied, rectify this situation by selecting the Copy Cells command on the AutoFill Options shortcut menu.

Inserting special symbols

Excel makes it easy to enter special symbols, such as foreign currency indicators, and special characters, such as the trademark and copyright symbols, into your cell entries. To add a special symbol or character to a cell entry you're making or editing, click Insert⇨Symbol on the Ribbon or press Alt+NU to open the Symbol dialog box (similar to the one shown in Figure 2-11).

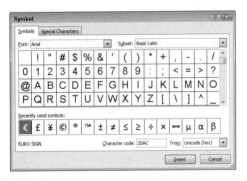

Figure 2-11: Use the Symbol dialog box to insert special symbols and characters into your cell entries.

The Symbol dialog box contains two tabs: Symbols and Special Characters. To insert a mathematical or foreign currency symbol on the Symbols tab, click its symbol in the list box and then click the Insert button. (You can also double-click the symbol.) To insert characters, such as foreign language or accented characters from other character sets, click the Subset drop-down button, click the name of the set in the drop-down list, and then click the desired characters in the list box. You can also insert commonly used currency and mathematical symbols, such as the pound or plus-or-minus symbol, by clicking them in the Recently Used Symbols section at the bottom of this tab.

To insert special characters, such as the registered trademark, paragraph symbol, and ellipsis, click the Special Characters tab of the Symbol dialog box, locate the symbol in the scrolling list, click it, and then click the Insert button. (You can insert one of these special characters by double-clicking it also.)

When you finish inserting special symbols and characters, close the Symbol dialog box by clicking its Close button in its upper-right corner.

Making Formulas Function Better

Earlier in this chapter, I show you how to create formulas that perform a series of simple mathematical operations, such as addition, subtraction, multiplication, and division. Instead of creating complex formulas from scratch out of an intricate combination of these operations, you can find an Excel function to get the job done.

A *function* is a predefined formula that performs a particular type of computation. All you have to do to use a function is supply the values that the function uses

when performing its calculations. As with simple formulas, you can enter the arguments for most functions either as a numerical value (for example, **22** or
–4.56) or, as is more common, as a cell reference
(**B10**) or as a cell range (**C3:F3**).

Just as with a formula you build yourself, each function you use must start with an equal sign (=) so that
Excel knows to enter the function as a formula rather
than as text. Following the equal sign, you enter the
name of the function (in uppercase or lowercase — it
doesn't matter, as long as you spell the name correctly). Following the name of the function, you enter
the arguments required to perform the calculations.
All function arguments are enclosed in a pair of
parentheses.

If you type the function directly in a cell, remember not to insert spaces between the equal sign,
function name, and the arguments enclosed in
parentheses. Some functions use more than one
value when performing their designated calculations. When this is the case, you separate each
function with a comma (not a space).

After you type the equal sign and begin typing the
first few letters of the name of the function you want
to use, a drop-down list showing all the functions that
begin with the letters you've typed appears immediately beneath the cell. When you see the name of the
function you want to use on this list, double-click it,
and Excel will finish entering the function name in the
cell and on the Formula bar as well as add the left
parenthesis that marks the beginning of the arguments for the function.

Excel then displays all the arguments that the function takes beneath the cell, and you can indicate any
cell or cell range that you want to use as the first
argument by either pointing to it or typing its cell or

range references. When the function uses more than one argument, you can point to the cells or cell ranges or enter the addresses for the second argument right after you enter a comma (,) to complete the first argument.

After you finish entering the last argument, you need to close off the function by typing a right parenthesis to mark the end of the argument list. The display of the function name, along with the arguments that appeared beneath the cell when you first selected the function from the drop-down list, disappear. Click the Enter button or press Enter (or the appropriate arrow key) to insert the function into the cell and have Excel calculate the answer.

Inserting a function into a formula

You can enter a function by typing it directly in a cell; however, Excel provides an Insert Function button on the Formula bar that enables you to select any of Excel's functions. When you click this button, Excel opens the Insert Function dialog box (shown in Figure 2-12) where you can select the function you want to use. After you select your function, Excel opens the Function Arguments dialog box. In this dialog box, you specify the function arguments. The real boon comes when you're fooling with an unfamiliar function or one that's kind of complex. You can get loads of help in completing the argument text boxes in the Function Arguments dialog box by clicking the Help on This Function link in the lower-left corner.

The Insert Function dialog box contains three boxes: a Search for a Function text box, an Or Select a Category drop-down list box, and a Select a Function list box. When you open the Insert Function dialog box, Excel automatically selects Most Recently Used

as the category in the Select a Category drop-down
list box and displays the functions you usually use in
the Select a Function list box.

Figure 2-12: Select the function you want to use in the Insert
Function dialog box.

If your function isn't among the most recently used,
you must select the appropriate category of your
function in the Select a Category drop-down list box.
If you don't know the category, you must search for
the function by typing a description of its purpose in
the Search for a Function text box and then pressing
Enter or clicking the Go button. For example, to locate
all the Excel functions that total values, you enter
total in the Search for Function list box and click the
Go button. Excel displays its list of recommended
functions for calculating totals in the Select a
Function list box. You can peruse the recommended
functions by selecting each one. While you select
each function in this list, the Insert Function dialog
box shows you the required arguments followed by a
description, at the bottom of the dialog box, of what
the function does.

After you locate and select the function you want to use, click the OK button to insert the function into the current cell and open the Function Arguments dialog box. This dialog box displays the required arguments for the function along with any that are optional. For example, suppose that you select the SUM function (the crown jewel of the Most Recently Used function category) in the Select a Function list box and then click OK. As soon as you do, the program inserts

```
SUM()
```

in the current cell and on the Formula bar (following the equal sign), and the Function Arguments dialog box showing the SUM arguments appears on the screen (as shown in Figure 2-13). This is where you add the arguments for the SUM function.

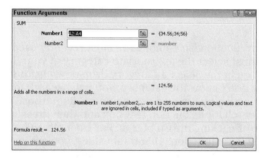

Figure 2-13: Specify the arguments to use in the selected function in the Function Arguments dialog box.

As shown in Figure 2-13, you can sum up to 255 numbers in the Function Arguments dialog box. What's not obvious, however, is that these numbers don't have to be in single cells. In fact, most of the time you'll be selecting a whole slew of numbers in nearby cells (in a multiple cell selection) that you want to total.

To select your first number argument in the dialog box, you click the cell (or drag through the block of cells) in the worksheet while the insertion point is in the Number1 text box. Excel then displays the cell address (or range address) in the Number1 text box while, at the same time, showing the value in the cell (or values, if you select a bunch of cells) in the box to the right. Excel displays the total near the bottom of the Function Arguments dialog box after the words *Formula result=*.

When selecting cells, you can minimize this arguments dialog box to just the contents of the Number1 text box by dragging the cell pointer through the cells to sum in the worksheet. After you minimize the arguments dialog box while selecting the cells for the first argument, you can then expand it again by releasing the mouse button.

You can also reduce the dialog box to the Number1 argument text box by clicking the Minimize Dialog Box button on the right of the text box, selecting the cells, and then clicking the Maximize Dialog Box button (the only button displayed on the far right) or by pressing the Esc key. Instead of minimizing the dialog box, you can also temporarily move it out of the way by clicking on any part and then dragging the dialog box to its new destination on the screen.

If you're adding more than one cell (or bunch of cells) in a worksheet, press the Tab key or click the Number2 text box to move the insertion point to that text box. (Excel responds by extending the argument list with a Number3 text box.) Here is where you specify the second cell (or cell range) to add to the one now showing in the Number1 text box. After you click the cell or drag through the second cell range, the program displays the cell address(es), the numbers in the cell(s) to the right, and the running total near the bottom of the Function Arguments dialog box after

Formula result= (as shown in Figure 2-13). You can minimize the entire Function Arguments dialog box down to just the contents of the argument text box you're dealing with (Number2, Number3, and so on) by clicking its particular Minimize Dialog Box button if the dialog box obscures the cells that you need to select.

When you finish pointing out the cells or bunch of cells to sum, click the OK button to close the Function Arguments dialog box and put the SUM function in the current cell.

I'd be totally lost without AutoSum

Before leaving this fascinating discussion on entering functions, I want you to get to the AutoSum tool in the Editing group on the Home tab of the Ribbon. Look for the Greek sigma (Σ) symbol. This little tool is worth its weight in gold. In addition to entering the SUM, AVERAGE, COUNT, MAX, or MIN functions, it also selects the most likely range of cells in the current column or row that you want to use as the function's argument and then automatically enters them as the function's argument. Nine times out of ten, Excel selects (with the *marquee* or moving dotted line) the correct cell range to total, average, count, and so forth. For that tenth case, you can manually correct the range by simply dragging the cell pointer through the block of cells to sum.

Simply click the AutoSum button on the Home tab when you want to insert the SUM function into the current cell. If you want to use this button to insert another function, such as AVERAGE, COUNT, MAX, or MIN, you need to click its drop-down button and select the name of the desired function on its pop-up menu (click Count Numbers on the menu to insert the

COUNT function). If you select the More Functions command on this menu, Excel opens the Insert Function dialog box as though you had clicked the *fx* button on the Formula bar.

In Figure 2-14, check out how to use the AutoSum tool to total the sales of Jack Sprat Diet Centers in row 3. Position the cell pointer in cell E3 where the first-quarter total is to appear and then click the AutoSum tool. Excel inserts SUM (equal sign and all) onto the Formula bar; places a marquee around the cells B3, C3, and D3; and uses the cell range B3:D3 as the argument of the SUM function.

	SUM	▾	× ✔ *fx*	=SUM(B3:D3)			
	A	B	C	D	E	F	G
1	Mother Goose Enterprises - 2010 Sales						
2		Jan	Feb	Mar	Qtr 1		
3	Jack Sprat Diet Centers	80138.58	59389.56	19960.06	=SUM(B3:D3)		
4	Jack and Jill Trauma Centers	12345.62	89645.7	25436.84	SUM(**number1**, [number2], …)		
5	Mother Hubbard Dog Goodies	12657.05	60593.56	42300.28			
6	Rub-a-Dub-Dub Tubs and Spas	17619.79	40635	42814.99			
7	Georgie Porgie Pudding Pies	57133.56	62926.31	12408.75			
8	Hickory, Dickory, Doc Clock Repair	168591	124718.1	4196.13			
9	Little Bo Peep Pet Detectives	30834.63	71111.25	74926.24			
10	Total						
11							
12							
13							
14							
15							

Figure 2-14: To total Jack Sprat Diet Centers first-quarter sales for row 3, click the AutoSum button in cell E3 and press Enter.

Now look at the worksheet after you insert the function in cell E3 (see Figure 2-15). The calculated total appears in cell E3 while the following SUM function formula appears in the Formula bar:

```
=SUM(B3:D3)
```

	A	B	C	D	E	F
	E3	▼	⨍ₓ =SUM(B3:D3)			
1	Mother Goose Enterprises - 2010 Sales					
2		Jan	Feb	Mar	Qtr 1	
3	Jack Sprat Diet Centers	80138.58	59389.56	19960.06	159488.2	
4	Jack and Jill Trauma Centers	12345.62	89645.7	25436.84		
5	Mother Hubbard Dog Goodies	12657.05	60593.56	42300.28		
6	Rub-a-Dub-Dub Tubs and Spas	17619.79	40635	42814.99		
7	Georgie Porgie Pudding Pies	57133.56	62926.31	12408.75		
8	Hickory, Dickory, Doc Clock Repair	168591	124718.1	4196.13		
9	Little Bo Peep Pet Detectives	30834.63	71111.25	74926.24		
10	Total					
11						
12						
13						
14						
15						

Figure 2-15: The worksheet with the first-quarter totals calculated with AutoSum.

After entering the function to total the sales of Jack Sprat Diet Centers, you can copy this formula to total sales for the rest of the companies by dragging the fill handle down column E until the cell range E3:E10 is highlighted.

Look at Figure 2-16 to see how you can use the AutoSum tool to total the January sales for all the Mother Goose Enterprises in column B. Position the cell pointer in cell B10 where you want the total to appear. Click the AutoSum tool, and Excel places the marquee around cells B3 through B9 and correctly enters the cell range B3:B9 as the argument of the SUM function.

In Figure 2-17, you see the worksheet after inserting the function in cell B10 and using the AutoFill feature to copy the formula to cells C10 and D10 to the right. (To use AutoFill, drag the fill handle through the cells to the right until you reach cell D10. Release the mouse button.)

	SUM	▾ (● ✗ ✓ ƒx)	=SUM(B3:B9)			
⊿	A	B	C	D	E	F
1	Mother Goose Enterprises - 2010 Sales					
2		Jan	Feb	Mar	Qtr 1	
3	Jack Sprat Diet Centers	80138.58	59389.56	19960.06	159488.2	
4	Jack and Jill Trauma Centers	12345.62	89645.7	25436.84	127428.2	
5	Mother Hubbard Dog Goodies	12657.05	60593.56	42300.28	115550.9	
6	Rub-a-Dub-Dub Tubs and Spas	17619.79	40635	42814.99	101069.8	
7	Georgie Porgie Pudding Pies	57133.56	62926.31	12408.75	132468.6	
8	Hickory, Dickory, Doc Clock Repair	168591	124718.1	4196.13	297505.2	
9	Little Bo Peep Pet Detectives	30834.63	71111.25	74926.24	176872.1	
10	Total	=SUM(B3:B9)				0
11		SUM(**number1**, [number2], ...)				
12						
13						
14						
15						

Figure 2-16: Click the AutoSum button in cell B10 and press Enter to total the January sales for all companies in column B.

	B10	▾ (●)	ƒx	=SUM(B3:B9)		
⊿	A	B	C	D	E	F
1	Mother Goose Enterprises - 2010 Sales					
2		Jan	Feb	Mar	Qtr 1	
3	Jack Sprat Diet Centers	80138.58	59389.56	19960.06	159488.2	
4	Jack and Jill Trauma Centers	12345.62	89645.7	25436.84	127428.2	
5	Mother Hubbard Dog Goodies	12657.05	60593.56	42300.28	115550.9	
6	Rub-a-Dub-Dub Tubs and Spas	17619.79	40635	42814.99	101069.8	
7	Georgie Porgie Pudding Pies	57133.56	62926.31	12408.75	132468.6	
8	Hickory, Dickory, Doc Clock Repair	168591	124718.1	4196.13	297505.2	
9	Little Bo Peep Pet Detectives	30834.63	71111.25	74926.24	176872.1	
10	Total	379320.2	509019.5	222043.3	1110383	
11						
12						
13						
14						
15						

Figure 2-17: The worksheet after copying the SUM function formulas using the fill handle.

Making Sure Your Data Is Safe

All the work you do in any of the worksheets in your workbook is at risk until you save the workbook as a disk file, normally on your computer's hard drive. Should you lose power or should your computer crash for any reason before you save the workbook, you're out of luck. You have to re-create each keystroke — a painful task, made all the worse because it's so unnecessary. To avoid this unpleasantness altogether, adopt this motto: Save your work any time you enter more information than you could possibly bear to lose.

To encourage frequent saving on your part, Excel even provides you with a Save button on the Quick Access toolbar (the one with the picture of a 3.5" floppy disk, the very first on the toolbar). You don't even have to take the time and trouble to choose the Save command from the File pull-down menu (opened by choosing File) or even press Ctrl+S; you can simply click this button whenever you want to save new work.

When you click the Save button, press Ctrl+S, or choose File➪Save for the first time, Excel displays the Save As dialog box. Use this dialog box to replace the temporary document name (Book1, Book2, and so forth) with a more descriptive filename in the File Name text box, select a new file format in the Save As Type drop-down list box, and select a new drive and folder before you save the workbook as a disk file.

When you finish making changes in the Save As dialog box, click the Save button or press Enter to have Excel 2010 save your work. When Excel saves your workbook file, the program saves all the information in every worksheet in your workbook (including the last position of the cell cursor) in the designated folder and drive.

You don't have to fool with the Save As dialog box again unless you want to rename the workbook or save a copy of it in a different folder. If you want to do these things, you must choose File➪Save As or press Alt+FA to choose the Save As command rather than clicking the Save button on the Quick Access toolbar or pressing Ctrl+S.

The Save As dialog box in Windows 7 and Windows Vista

Figure 2-18 shows you the Save As dialog box as it appears in Excel 2010 when running the program under Windows 7. Here, you can replace the temporary filename (Book1, Book2, and so on) with a more descriptive name by clicking the File Name text box and typing in the new name (up to 255 characters total, including spaces).

Figure 2-18: The Save As dialog box enables you to select the filename and folder for the new workbook file as well as add tags to it.

To select a new folder in which to save the new workbook file, follow these steps:

1. In the Navigation Pane, click the name of the folder in the Favorites, Libraries, Computer, or Network section in which you want to save the workbook file.

2. To save the workbook file within a subfolder of one of the folders now displayed in the main pane of the Save As dialog box, double-click its folder icon to open it up.

3. (Optional) If you want to save the workbook file inside a new subfolder within the folder currently open in the Save As dialog box, click the New Folder button on the toolbar, replace the suggested New Folder name by typing the actual name of the folder, and then press Enter.

4. Click the Save button to save the file in the selected folder.

When the Save As dialog box is expanded by clicking the Browse Folders button, you can modify the authors or add tags to the new workbook file by clicking the Add an Author or Add a Tag text boxes. You can then use this information later when searching for the workbook. (See Chapter 3 for details on searching.)

Chapter 3

Editing a Spreadsheet

- -

In This Chapter

▶ Opening workbook files for editing

▶ Undoing your boo-boos

▶ Moving and copying with drag and drop

▶ Copying formulas

▶ Moving and copying with Cut, Copy, and Paste

▶ Deleting cell entries

▶ Deleting and inserting columns and rows

- -

*P*icture this: You just finished creating, formatting, and printing a major project with Excel — a workbook with your department's budget for the next fiscal year. Because you finally understand a little bit about how the Excel thing works, you finish the job in crack time. You're actually ahead of schedule.

You turn the workbook over to your boss so that she can check the numbers. With plenty of time for making those inevitable last-minute corrections, you're feeling on top of this situation.

Then comes the reality check — your boss brings the document back, and she's plainly agitated. "We forgot to include the estimates for the temps and our over-time hours. They go right here. While you're adding them, can you move these rows of figures up and those columns over?"

As she continues to suggest improvements, your heart begins to sink. These modifications are in a different league than, "Let's change these column headings from bold to italic and add shading to that row of totals." Clearly, you're looking at making structural changes that threaten to unravel the very fabric of your beautiful worksheet.

As the preceding fable points out, editing a worksheet in a workbook can occur on different levels:

- ✔ You can make changes that affect the contents of the cells, such as copying a row of column headings or moving a table to a new area in a particular worksheet.

- ✔ You can make changes that affect the structure of a worksheet itself, such as inserting new columns or rows (so that you can enter new data originally left out) or deleting unnecessary columns or rows from an existing table so that you don't leave any gaps.

- ✔ You can even make changes to the number of worksheets in a workbook (by either adding or deleting sheets).

In this chapter, you discover how to make these types of changes safely to a workbook.

Opening the Workbook for Editing

Before you can do any damage — I mean, make any changes — in a workbook, you have to open it up in Excel. To open a workbook, you can choose File➪Open, press Alt+FO, or use the old standby keyboard shortcuts Ctrl+O or Ctrl+F12.

Operating the Open dialog box

If you're running Excel 2010 under Windows 7, an Open dialog box very much like the one in Figure 3-1 appears. This dialog box is divided into panes: the Navigation pane on the left where you can select a new folder to open and the main pane on the right showing the icons for all the subfolders in the current folder as well as the documents that Excel can open.

The folder with contents displayed in the Open dialog box is either the one designated as the Default File Location on the Save tab of the Excel Options dialog box or the folder you last opened during your current Excel work session. If you haven't changed the default folder location since installing Excel 2010 on your computer, this default folder is the Documents Library (simply referred to as Documents in Windows Vista).

If you're running Excel 2010 on Windows Vista, your Open dialog box is similar to the one shown in Figure 3-1 except that your Navigation pane contains a Folders item instead of Libraries under your list of Favorites. Additionally, the Views button appears between the Organize and New Folder buttons and not to their right above the Navigation and main panes.

Change your view

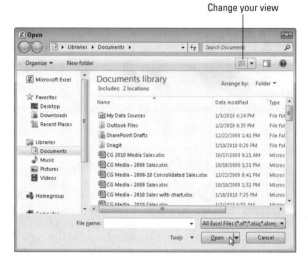

Figure 3-1: Use the Open dialog box to find and open a workbook for editing.

To open a workbook in another folder, click its link in the Favorite Links section of the Navigation pane or click the Expand Folders button (the one with the triangle pointing upward) and click its folder in this list.

If you open a new folder and it appears empty of all files (and you know that it's not an empty folder), this just means the folder doesn't contain any of the types of files that Excel can open directly (such as workbooks, template files, and macro sheets). To display all the files whether or not Excel can open them directly (meaning without some sort of conversion), click the drop-down button that appears next to the drop-down list box that currently displays All Excel Files and then click All Files on its drop-down menu.

When the icon for the workbook file you want to work with appears in the Open dialog box, you can then open it either by clicking its file icon and then clicking the Open button or, if you're handy with the mouse, by just double-clicking the file icon.

 You can use the slider attached to the Views drop-down list button in the Open dialog box to change the way folder and file icons appear in the dialog box. When you select Large Icons or Extra Large Icons on this slider (or anywhere in between), the Excel workbook icons actually show a preview of the data in the upper-left corner of the first worksheet when the file is saved with the preview picture option turned on:

✔ To enable the preview feature when saving workbooks in Excel 2010, select the Save Thumbnail check box in the Save As dialog box before saving the file for the first time.

✔ To enable the preview feature when saving workbooks in Excel 97 through 2003, click the Save Preview Picture check box on the Summary tab of the workbook's Properties dialog box (File➪Properties) before saving the file for the first time.

This preview of part of the first sheet can help you quickly identify the workbook you want to open for editing or printing.

Opening more than one workbook at a time

If you know that you're going to edit more than one of the workbook files shown in the list box of the Open dialog box, you can select multiple files in the list box.

Excel will then open all of them (in the order they're listed) when you click the Open button or press Enter.

 Remember that in order to select multiple files that appear sequentially in the Open dialog box, you click the first filename and then hold down the Shift key while you click the last filename. To select files that aren't listed sequentially, you need to hold down the Ctrl key while you click the various filenames.

After the workbook files are open in Excel, you can then switch documents by selecting their filename buttons on the Windows taskbar or by using the Flip feature (Alt+Tab) to select the workbook's thumbnail.

Opening recently edited workbooks

If you know that the workbook you now need to edit is one of those that you opened recently, you don't even have to fool around with the Open dialog box. Just choose File⇨Recent to display a Recent Workbooks list to the right of the pull-down menu (or press Alt+FR) and then click the name of the workbook to open for editing.

 When you open the Recent Workbooks list by pressing Alt+FR, Excel displays the number hot keys next to each of the recently opened spreadsheet files in the list. You then can open the one you need to edit simply by typing its number.

Excel 2010 automatically keeps a running list of the last 20 files you opened in the Recent Workbooks list on the File tab. If you want, you can have Excel display more or fewer files in this list on the File tab.

To change the number of recently opened files that appear, follow these simple steps:

1. **Choose File⇨Options⇨Advanced or press Alt+FIA to open the Advanced tab of the Excel Options dialog box.**

2. **Type a new entry (between 1 and 50) in the Show This Number of Recent Documents text box or use the spinner buttons to increase or decrease this number.**

3. **Click OK or press Enter to close the Excel Options dialog box.**

 Select the Quickly Access This Number of Recent Workbooks check box on the Recent Workbooks panel in the Backstage View to have Excel display the four most recently opened workbooks as items on the File tab. That way, you can open any of them by clicking its button without having to open the Recent Workbooks panel. After selecting the Quickly Access This Number of Recent Workbooks check box, you change the number of recently opened workbooks added to the File tab by entering the new number in its text box or selecting the number with its spinner buttons.

Searching for a workbook

The only problem you can encounter in opening a document from the Open dialog box is locating the filename. Everything's hunky-dory as long as you can see the workbook filename listed in the Open dialog box or know which folder to open in order to display it. But what about those times when a file seems to migrate mysteriously and can't be found on your computer?

When you run Excel 2010 under Windows 7 or Vista, the operating system adds a Search Documents text box (simply called Search in Vista) to the Open dialog box (see Figure 3-2). You can use this text box to search for missing workbooks from within the Open dialog box.

To find a missing workbook, click this search text box in the upper-right corner of the Open dialog box and then begin typing characters used in the workbook's filename or contained in the workbook itself.

As Windows finds any matches for the characters you type, the names of the workbook files (and other Excel files such as templates and macro sheets as well) appear in the Open dialog box. As soon as the workbook you want to open is listed, you can open it by clicking its icon and filename followed by the Open button or by double-clicking it.

Figure 3-2: Use the Search Documents text box in the Open dialog box to quickly search for any Excel workbook on your computer.

Opening files with a twist

The drop-down button attached to the Open command button at the bottom of the Open dialog box enables you to open the selected workbook file(s) in a special way, including:

- ✔ **Open Read-Only:** This command opens the files you select in the Open dialog box's list box in a read-only state, which means that you can look but you can't touch. (Actually, you can touch; you just can't save your changes.) To save changes in a read-only file, you must use the Save As command (File⇨Save As or Alt+FA) and give the workbook file a new filename. (Refer to Chapter 2.)

- ✔ **Open as Copy:** This command opens a copy of the files you select in the Open dialog box. Use this method of opening files as a safety net: If you mess up the copies, you always have the originals to fall back on.

- ✔ **Open in Browser:** This command opens work-book files you save as web pages in your favor-ite web browser. This command isn't available unless the program identifies that the selected file or files were saved as web pages rather than plain old Excel workbook files.

- ✔ **Open in Protected View:** This command opens the workbook file in Protected View mode that keeps you from making any changes to the con-tents of its worksheets until you click the Enable Editing button that appears in the orange Protected View panel at the top of the screen.

- ✔ **Open and Repair:** This command attempts to repair corrupted workbook files before opening them in Excel. When you select this command, a dialog box appears giving you a choice between attempting to repair the corrupted file or open-ing the recovered version, extracting data from the corrupted file, and placing it in a new work-book (which you can save with the Save com-mand). Click the Repair button to attempt to recover and open the file. Click the Extract Data button if you tried unsuccessfully to have Excel repair the file.

Much Ado about Undo

Before you start tearing into the workbook that you just opened, get to know the Undo feature, including how it can put right many of the things that you could inadvertently mess up. The Undo command button on the Quick Access toolbar is a regular chameleon button. When you delete the cell selection by pressing the Delete key, the Undo button's ScreenTip reads Undo Clear (Ctrl+Z). If you move some entries to a new part of the worksheet by dragging it, the Undo command button ScreenTip changes to Undo Drag and Drop (Ctrl+Z).

In addition to clicking the Undo command button (in whatever guise it appears), you can also choose this command by pressing Ctrl+Z (perhaps for *unZap*).

The Undo command button on the Quick Access toolbar changes in response to whatever action you just took; that is, it changes after each action. If you forget to strike when the iron is hot, so to speak, and don't use the Undo feature to restore the worksheet to its previous state *before* you choose another command, you then need to consult the drop-down menu on the Undo button. Click its drop-down button that appears to the right of the Undo icon (the curved arrow pointing to the left). After the Undo drop-down menu appears, click the action on this menu that you want undone. Excel will then undo this action and all actions that precede it in the list (which are selected automatically).

Undo is Redo the second time around

After using the Undo command button on the Quick Access toolbar, Excel 2010 activates the Redo command button to its immediate right. If you delete an entry from a cell by pressing the Delete key and then click the Undo command button or press Ctrl+Z, the ScreenTip that appears when you position the mouse pointer over the Redo command button reads Redo Clear (Ctrl+Y).

When you click the Redo command button or press Ctrl+Y, Excel redoes the thing you just undid. Actually, this sounds more complicated than it is. It simply means that you use Undo to switch between the result of an action and the state of the worksheet just before that action until you decide how you want the worksheet (or until the cleaning crew turns off the lights and locks up the building).

What to do when you can't Undo

I feel that I have to tell you that Undo doesn't work all the time! Although you can undo your latest erroneous cell deletion, bad move, or unwise copy, you can't undo your latest rash save. (You know, like when you meant to choose Save As from the File tab to save the edited worksheet under a different document name but chose Save and ended up saving the changes as part of the current document.)

Unfortunately, Excel doesn't let you know when you are about to take a step from which there is no return — until it's too late. After you've gone and done the un-undoable and you click the Undo button where you expect its ScreenTip to say Undo *blah, blah*, it now reads Can't Undo.

One exception to this rule is when the program gives you advance warning (which you should heed). When you choose a command that is normally possible but because you're low on memory or the change will affect so much of the worksheet, or both, Excel knows that it can't undo the change if it goes through with it, the program displays an alert box telling you that there isn't enough memory to undo this action and asking whether you want to go ahead anyway. If you click the Yes button and complete the edit, realize that you do so without any possibility of pardon. If you find out, too late, that you deleted a row of essential formulas (that you forgot about because you couldn't see them), you can't bring them back with Undo. In such a case, you would have to close the file (File⇨Close) and *NOT save your changes*.

Doing the Old Drag-and-Drop

The first editing technique you need to learn is *drag and drop*. As the name implies, you can use this mouse technique to pick up a cell selection and drop it into a new place on the worksheet. Although drag and drop is primarily a technique for moving cell entries around a worksheet, you can adapt it to copy a cell selection, as well.

To use drag and drop to move a range of cell entries (one cell range at a time), follow these steps:

1. **Select a cell range.**

2. **Position the mouse pointer on one edge of the extended cell cursor that now surrounds the entire cell range.**

   Your signal that you can start dragging the cell range to its new position in the worksheet is when the pointer changes to the arrowhead.

3. **Drag your selection to its destination.**

   Drag your selection by depressing and holding down the primary mouse button — usually the left one — while moving the mouse.

   While you drag your selection, you actually move only the outline of the cell range, and Excel keeps you informed of what the new cell range address would be (as a kind of drag-and-drop ScreenTip) if you were to release the mouse button at that location.

   Drag the outline until it's positioned where you want the entries to appear (as evidenced by the cell range in the drag-and-drop ScreenTip).

4. **Release the mouse button.**

   The cell entries within that range reappear in the new location as soon as you release the mouse button.

In Figures 3-3 and 3-4, I show how you can drag and drop a cell range. In Figure 3-3, I select the cell range A10:E10 (containing the quarterly totals) to move it to row 12 to make room for sales figures for two new companies (Simple Simon Pie Shoppes and Jack Be Nimble Candlesticks, which hadn't been acquired when this workbook was first created). In Figure 3-4, you see the Mother Goose Enterprises – 2010 Sales worksheet right after completing this move.

The arguments for the SUM functions in cell range B13:E13 do not keep pace with the change — it continues to sum only the values in rows 3 through 9 after the move. However, when you enter the sales figures for these new enterprises in columns B through C in rows 10, 11, and 12, Excel shows off its smarts and updates the formulas in row 13 to include the new entries. For example, the SUM(B3:B9) formula in B13 magically becomes SUM(B3:B12).

	A	B	C	D	E	F
1	Mother Goose Enterprises - 2010 Sales					
2		Jan	Feb	Mar	Qtr 1	
3	Jack Sprat Diet Centers	80,138.58	59,389.56	19,960.06	$ 159,488.20	
4	Jack and Jill Trauma Centers	12,345.62	89,645.70	25,436.84	$ 127,428.16	
5	Mother Hubbard Dog Goodies	12,657.05	60,593.56	42,300.28	$ 115,550.89	
6	Rub-a-Dub-Dub Tubs and Spas	17,619.79	40,635.00	42,814.99	$ 101,069.78	
7	Georgie Porgie Pudding Pies	57,133.56	62,926.31	12,408.75	$ 132,468.62	
8	Hickory, Dickory, Doc Clock Repair	168,591.00	124,718.10	4,196.13	$ 297,505.23	
9	Little Bo Peep Pet Detectives	30,834.63	71,111.25	74,926.24	$ 176,872.12	
10	Total	$379,320.23	$509,019.48	$222,043.29	$1,110,383.00	
11						
12						
13						
14						

Figure 3-3: Dragging the cell selection to its new position in a worksheet.

	A	B	C	D	E	F
1	Mother Goose Enterprises - 2010 Sales					
2		Jan	Feb	Mar	Qtr 1	
3	Jack Sprat Diet Centers	80,138.58	59,389.56	19,960.06	$ 159,488.20	
4	Jack and Jill Trauma Centers	12,345.62	89,645.70	25,436.84	$ 127,428.16	
5	Mother Hubbard Dog Goodies	12,657.05	60,593.56	42,300.28	$ 115,550.89	
6	Rub-a-Dub-Dub Tubs and Spas	17,619.79	40,635.00	42,814.99	$ 101,069.78	
7	Georgie Porgie Pudding Pies	57,133.56	62,926.31	12,408.75	$ 132,468.62	
8	Hickory, Dickory, Doc Clock Repair	168,591.00	124,718.10	4,196.13	$ 297,505.23	
9	Little Bo Peep Pet Detectives	30,834.63	71,111.25	74,926.24	$ 176,872.12	
10						
11						
12	Total		$379,320.23	$509,019.48	$222,043.29	$1,110,383.00
13						
14						
15						

Figure 3-4: A worksheet after dropping the cell selection into its new place.

Copies, drag-and-drop style

What if you want to copy rather than drag and drop a cell range? Suppose that you need to start a new table in rows farther down the worksheet, and you want to copy the cell range with the formatted title and column headings for the new table. To copy the formatted title range in the sample worksheet, follow these steps:

1. **Select the cell range.**

   In the case of Figures 3-3 and 3-4, that's cell range A1:E2.

2. **Hold the Ctrl key down while you position the mouse pointer on an edge of the selection (that is, the expanded cell cursor).**

   The pointer changes from a thick shaded cross to an arrowhead with a + (plus sign) to the right of it with the drag-and-drop ScreenTip beside it. The plus sign next to the pointer is your signal that drag and drop will *copy* the selection rather than *move* it.

3. **Drag the cell-selection outline to the place where you want the copy to appear and release the mouse button.**

Insertions courtesy of drag and drop

Like the Klingons of *Star Trek* fame, spreadsheets, such as Excel, never take prisoners. When you place or move a new entry into an occupied cell, the new entry completely replaces the old as though the old entry never existed in that cell.

To insert the cell range you're moving or copying within a populated region of the worksheet without wiping out existing entries, hold down the Shift key while you drag the selection. (If you're copying, you have to get ambitious and hold down both the Shift and Ctrl keys at the same time!)

With the Shift key depressed while you drag, instead of a rectangular outline of the cell range, you get an I-beam shape that shows where the selection will be inserted if you release the mouse button along with the address of the cell range (as a kind of Insertion ScreenTip). When you move the I-beam shape, notice that it wants to attach itself to the column and row borders while you move it. After you position the l-beam at the column or row border where you want to insert the cell range, release the mouse button. Excel inserts the cell range, moving the existing entries to neighboring blank cells (out of harm's way).

Formulas on AutoFill

Copying with drag and drop (by holding down the Ctrl key) is useful when you need to copy a bunch of neighboring cells to a new part of the worksheet. Frequently, however, you just need to copy a single formula that you just created to a bunch of neighboring cells that need to perform the same type of calculation (such as totaling columns of figures). This type of formula copy, although quite common, can't be done with drag and drop. Instead, use the AutoFill feature (read about this in Chapter 2) or the Copy and Paste commands. (See the section "Cut and paste, digital style" later in this chapter.)

Here's how you can use AutoFill to copy one formula to a range of cells. In Figure 3-5, you can see the Mother Goose Enterprises – 2010 Sales worksheet with all the companies, but this time with only one monthly total in row 12, which is in the process of being copied through cell E12.

	A	B	C	D	E	F
	B12	▾	*fx*	=SUM(B3:B11)		
1	Mother Goose Enterprises - 2010 Sales					
2		Jan	Feb	Mar	Qtr 1	
3	Jack Sprat Diet Centers	80,138.58	59,389.56	19,960.06	$ 159,488.20	
4	Jack and Jill Trauma Centers	12,345.62	89,645.70	25,436.84	$ 127,428.16	
5	Mother Hubbard Dog Goodies	12,657.05	60,593.56	42,300.28	$ 115,550.89	
6	Rub-a-Dub-Dub Tubs and Spas	17,619.79	40,635.00	42,814.99	$ 101,069.78	
7	Georgie Porgie Pudding Pies	57,133.56	62,926.31	12,408.75	$ 132,468.62	
8	Hickory, Dickory, Doc Clock Repair	168,591.00	124,718.10	4,196.13	$ 297,505.23	
9	Little Bo Peep Pet Detectives	30,834.63	71,111.25	74,926.24	$ 176,872.12	
10	Simple Simon Pie Shoppes	104,937.77	77,943.19	45,897.25	$ 228,778.21	
11	Jack-Be-Nimble Candlesticks	128,237.32	95,035.19	78,654.50	$ 301,927.01	
12	Total	$612,495.32				
13						
14						
15						

Figure 3-5: Copying a formula to a cell range with AutoFill.

Figure 3-6 shows the worksheet after dragging the fill handle in cell B12 to select the cell range C12:E12 (where this formula should be copied).

	A	B	C	D	E	F
	B12 ▾	*fx* =SUM(B3:B11)				
	A	B	C	D	E	F
1	Mother Goose Enterprises - 2010 Sales					
2		Jan	Feb	Mar	Qtr 1	
3	Jack Sprat Diet Centers	80,138.58	59,389.56	19,960.06	$ 159,488.20	
4	Jack and Jill Trauma Centers	12,345.62	89,645.70	25,436.84	$ 127,428.16	
5	Mother Hubbard Dog Goodies	12,657.05	60,593.56	42,300.28	$ 115,550.89	
6	Rub-a-Dub-Dub Tubs and Spas	17,619.79	40,635.00	42,814.99	$ 101,069.78	
7	Georgie Porgie Pudding Pies	57,133.56	62,926.31	12,408.75	$ 132,468.62	
8	Hickory, Dickory, Doc Clock Repair	168,591.00	124,718.10	4,196.13	$ 297,505.23	
9	Little Bo Peep Pet Detectives	30,834.63	71,111.25	74,926.24	$ 176,872.12	
10	Simple Simon Pie Shoppes	104,937.77	77,943.19	45,897.25	$ 228,778.21	
11	Jack-Be-Nimble Candlesticks	128,237.32	95,035.19	78,654.50	$ 301,927.01	
12	Total	$612,495.32	$681,997.86	$346,595.04	$1,641,088.22	
13						
14						
15						

Figure 3-6: The worksheet after copying the formula totaling the monthly (and quarterly) sales.

Relatively speaking

Figure 3-6 shows the worksheet after the formula in a cell is copied to the cell range C12:E12 and cell B12 is active. Notice how Excel handles the copying of formulas. The original formula in cell B12 is as follows:

```
=SUM(B3:B11)
```

When the original formula is copied to cell C12, Excel changes the formula slightly so that it looks like this:

```
=SUM(C3:C11)
```

Excel adjusts the column reference, changing it from B to C, because I copied from left to right across the rows.

When you copy a formula to a cell range that extends down the rows, Excel adjusts the row numbers in the copied formulas rather than the column letters to suit the position of each copy. For example, cell E3 in the Mother Goose Enterprises – 2010 Sales worksheet contains the following formula:

```
=SUM(B3:D3)
```

When you copy this formula to cell E4, Excel changes the copy of the formula to the following:

```
=SUM(B4:D4)
```

Excel adjusts the row reference to keep current with the new row 4 position. Because Excel adjusts the cell references in copies of a formula relative to the direction of the copying, the cell references are known as *relative cell references*.

Some things are absolutes!

All new formulas you create naturally contain relative cell references unless you say otherwise. Because most copies you make of formulas require adjustments of their cell references, you rarely have to give this arrangement a second thought. Then, every once in a while, you come across an exception that calls for limiting when and how cell references are adjusted in copies.

One of the most common of these exceptions is when you want to compare a range of different values with a single value, such as when you want to compute what percentage each part is to the total. For example, in the Mother Goose Enterprises – 2010 Sales worksheet, you encounter this situation in creating and copying a formula that calculates what percentage each monthly total (in the cell range B14:D14) is of the quarterly total in cell E12.

Suppose that you want to enter these formulas in row 14 of the Mother Goose Enterprises – 2010 Sales

worksheet, starting in cell B14. The formula in cell
B14 for calculating the percentage of the January-
sales-to-first-quarter-total is very straightforward:

```
=B12/E12
```

This formula divides the January sales total in cell
B12 by the quarterly total in E12 (what could be
easier?). Look, however, at what would happen if you
dragged the fill handle one cell to the right to copy
this formula to cell C14:

```
=C12/F12
```

The adjustment of the first cell reference from B12 to
C12 is just what the doctor ordered. However, the
adjustment of the second cell reference from E12 to
F12 is a disaster. Not only do you not calculate what
percentage the February sales in cell C12 are of the
first-quarter sales in E12, but you also end up with
one of those horrible #DIV/0! error things in cell C14.

To stop Excel from adjusting a cell reference in a formula in any copies you make, convert the cell reference from relative to absolute. You do this by
pressing the function key F4, after you put Excel in
Edit mode (F2). Excel indicates that you make the cell
reference absolute by placing dollar signs in front of
the column letter and row number. For example, in
Figure 3-7, cell B14 contains the correct formula to
copy to the cell range C14:D14:

```
=B12/$E$12
```

Look at the worksheet after this formula is copied to
the range C14:D14 with the fill handle and cell C14 is
selected (see Figure 3-8). Notice that the formula bar
shows that this cell contains the following formula:

```
=C12/$E$12
```

	A	B	C	D	E	F
	B14	▾	*fx*	=B12/$E$12		
1	Mother Goose Enterprises - 2010 Sales					
2		Jan	Feb	Mar	Qtr 1	
3	Jack Sprat Diet Centers	80,138.58	59,389.56	19,960.06	$ 159,488.20	
4	Jack and Jill Trauma Centers	12,345.62	89,645.70	25,436.84	$ 127,428.16	
5	Mother Hubbard Dog Goodies	12,657.05	60,593.56	42,300.28	$ 115,550.89	
6	Rub-a-Dub-Dub Tubs and Spas	17,619.79	40,635.00	42,814.99	$ 101,069.78	
7	Georgie Porgie Pudding Pies	57,133.56	62,926.31	12,408.75	$ 132,468.62	
8	Hickory, Dickory, Doc Clock Repair	168,591.00	124,718.10	4,196.13	$ 297,505.23	
9	Little Bo Peep Pet Detectives	30,834.63	71,111.25	74,926.24	$ 176,872.12	
10	Simple Simon Pie Shoppes	104,937.77	77,943.19	45,897.25	$ 228,778.21	
11	Jack-Be-Nimble Candlesticks	128,237.32	95,035.19	78,654.50	$ 301,927.01	
12	Total	$612,495.32	$681,997.86	$346,595.04	$1,641,088.22	
13						
14	Monthly/Qtrly Percentage	37%				
15					+	

Figure 3-7: Copying the formula for computing the ratio of monthly to quarterly sales with an absolute cell reference.

	A	B	C	D	E	F
	C14	▾	*fx*	=C12/$E$12		
1	Mother Goose Enterprises - 2010 Sales					
2		Jan	Feb	Mar	Qtr 1	
3	Jack Sprat Diet Centers	80,138.58	59,389.56	19,960.06	$ 159,488.20	
4	Jack and Jill Trauma Centers	12,345.62	89,645.70	25,436.84	$ 127,428.16	
5	Mother Hubbard Dog Goodies	12,657.05	60,593.56	42,300.28	$ 115,550.89	
6	Rub-a-Dub-Dub Tubs and Spas	17,619.79	40,635.00	42,814.99	$ 101,069.78	
7	Georgie Porgie Pudding Pies	57,133.56	62,926.31	12,408.75	$ 132,468.62	
8	Hickory, Dickory, Doc Clock Repair	168,591.00	124,718.10	4,196.13	$ 297,505.23	
9	Little Bo Peep Pet Detectives	30,834.63	71,111.25	74,926.24	$ 176,872.12	
10	Simple Simon Pie Shoppes	104,937.77	77,943.19	45,897.25	$ 228,778.21	
11	Jack-Be-Nimble Candlesticks	$128,237.32	95,035.19	$ 78,654.50	$ 301,927.01	
12	Total	$612,495.32	$681,997.86	$346,595.04	$1,641,088.22	
13						
14	Monthly/Qtrly Percentage	37%	42%	21%		
15						

Figure 3-8: The worksheet after copying the formula with the absolute cell reference.

Because E12 was changed to $E$12 in the original formula, all the copies have this same absolute (non-changing) reference.

Cut and paste, digital style

Instead of using drag and drop or AutoFill, you can use the old standby Cut, Copy, and Paste commands to move or copy information in a worksheet. These commands use the Office Clipboard as a kind of electronic halfway house where the information you cut or copy remains until you decide to paste it somewhere. Because of this Clipboard arrangement, you can use these commands to move or copy information to any other workbook open in Excel or even to other programs running in Windows (such as a Word 2010 document).

To move a cell selection with Cut and Paste, follow these steps:

1. **Select the cells you want to move.**

2. **Click the Cut command button in the Clipboard group on the Home tab (the button with the scissors icon).**

   If you prefer, you can choose Cut by pressing Ctrl+X.

3. **Move the cell cursor to the new range to which you want the information moved, or click the cell in the upper-left corner of the new range.**

4. **Press Enter to complete the move operation.**

   If you're feeling ambitious, click the Paste command button in the Clipboard group on the Home tab or press Ctrl+V.

Notice that when you indicate the destination range, you don't have to select a range of blank cells that matches the shape and size of the cell selection you're moving. Excel needs to know only the location of the cell in the upper-left corner of the destination range to figure out where to put the rest of the cells.

Copying a cell selection with the Copy and Paste commands follows an identical procedure to the one you use with the Cut and Paste commands. After selecting the range to copy, you can get the information into the Clipboard by clicking the Copy button on the

Ribbon's Home tab, choosing Copy from the cell's shortcut menu, or pressing Ctrl+C.

Paste it again, Sam . . .

An advantage to copying a selection with the Copy and Paste commands and the Clipboard is that you can paste the information multiple times. Just make sure that, instead of pressing Enter to complete the first copy operation, you click the Paste button on the Home tab of the Ribbon or press Ctrl+V.

When you use the Paste command to complete a copy operation, Excel copies the selection to the range you designate without removing the marquee from the original selection. This is your signal that you can select another destination range (in either the same or a different document).

After you select the first cell of the next range where you want the selection copied, choose the Paste command again. You can continue in this manner, pasting the same selection to your heart's content. When you make the last copy, press Enter instead of choosing the Paste command button or pressing Ctrl+V. If you forget and choose Paste, get rid of the marquee around the original cell range by pressing the Esc key.

Keeping pace with Paste Options

Right after you click the Paste button on the Home tab of the Ribbon or press Ctrl+V to paste cell entries that you copy (not cut) to the Clipboard, Excel displays a Paste Options button with the label, (Ctrl), to its immediate right at the end of the pasted range. When you click this drop-down button or press the Ctrl key, a palette similar to the one shown in Figure 3-9 appears with three groups of buttons (Paste, Paste Values, and Other Paste Options).

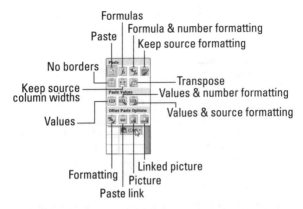

Figure 3-9: Clicking the Paste Options button or pressing the Ctrl key after completing a paste operation gives you this palette of paste options.

You can use these paste options to control or restrict the type of content and formatting that's included in the pasted cell range. The paste options (complete with the hot keys you can type to select them) on the Paste Options palette include:

- ✔ **Paste (P):** Excel pastes all the stuff in the cell selection (formulas, formatting, you name it).

- ✔ **Formulas (F):** Excel pastes all the text, numbers, and formulas in the current cell selection without their formatting.

- ✔ **Formulas & Number Formatting (O):** Excel pastes the number formats assigned to the copied values along with their formulas.

- ✔ **Keep Source Formatting (K):** Excel copies the formatting from the original cells and pastes the formatting into the destination cells (along with the copied entries).

✔ **No Borders (B):** Excel pastes all the stuff in the cell selection without copying any borders applied to its cell range.

✔ **Keep Source Column Widths (W):** Excel makes the width of the columns in the destination range the same as those in the source range when it copies their cell entries.

✔ **Transpose (T):** Excel changes the orientation of the pasted entries. For example, if the original cells' entries run down the rows of a single column of the worksheet, the transposed pasted entries will run across the columns of a single row.

✔ **Values (V):** Excel pastes only the calculated results of any formulas in the source cell range.

✔ **Values & Number Formatting (A):** Excel pastes the calculated results of any formulas along with all the formatting assigned to the labels, values, and formulas in the source cell range into the destination range. This means that all the labels and values in the destination range appear formatted just like the source range even though all the original formulas are lost and only the calculated values are retained.

✔ **Values & Source Formatting (E):** Excel pastes the calculated results of any formulas along with all formatting assigned to the source cell range.

✔ **Formatting (R):** Excel pastes only the formatting (and not the entries) copied from the source cell range to the destination range.

✔ **Paste Link (N):** Excel creates linking formulas in the destination range so that any changes that you make to the entries in cells in the source range are immediately brought forward and reflected in the corresponding cells of the destination range.

✔ **Picture (U):** Excel pastes only the pictures in the copied cell selection.

✔ **Linked Picture (I):** Excel pastes a link to the pictures in the copied cell selection.

What's so special about Paste Special?

Normally, unless you fool around with the Paste Options (see the preceding section), Excel copies all the information in the range of cells you selected: formatting, as well the formulas, text, and other values you enter. You can use the Paste Special command to specify which entries and formatting to use in the current paste operation. Many of the Paste Special options are also available on the Paste Options palette.

To paste particular parts of a cell selection while discarding others, click the drop-down button that appears at the bottom of the Paste command button on the Ribbon's Home tab. Then, click Paste Special on its drop-down menu to open the Paste Special dialog box shown in Figure 3-10.

The options in the Paste Special dialog box include

✔ **All** to paste all the stuff in the cell selection (formulas, formatting, you name it).

✔ **Formulas** to paste all the text, numbers, and formulas in the current cell selection without their formatting.

✔ **Values** to convert formulas in the current cell selection to their calculated values.

✔ **Formats** to paste only the formatting from the current cell selection, leaving the cell entries in the dust.

Figure 3-10: Use the options in the Paste Special dialog box to control what part of the copied cell selection to include in the paste operation.

> ✔ **Comments** to paste only the notes that you attach to their cells (kind of like electronic self-stick notes).

> ✔ **Validation** to paste only the data validation rules into the cell range that you set up with the Data Validation command (which enables you to set what value or range of values is allowed in a particular cell or cell range).

> ✔ **All Using Source Theme** to paste all the information plus the cell styles applied to the cells.

> ✔ **All Except Borders** to paste all the stuff in the cell selection without copying any borders you use there.

> ✔ **Column Widths** to apply the column widths of the cells copied to the Clipboard to the columns where the cells are pasted.

> ✔ **Formulas and Number Formats** to include the number formats assigned to the pasted values and formulas.

> ✔ **Values and Number Formats** to convert formulas to their calculated values and include the

number formats you assign to all the pasted values.

✔ **All Merging Conditional Formats** to paste Conditional Formatting into the cell range.

✔ **None** to have Excel perform no mathematical operation between the data entries you cut or copy to the Clipboard and the data entries in the cell range where you paste.

✔ **Add** to add the data you cut or copy to the Clipboard and the data entries in the cell range where you paste.

✔ **Subtract** to subtract the data you cut or copy to the Clipboard from the data entries in the cell range where you paste.

✔ **Multiply** to multiply the data you cut or copy to the Clipboard by the data entries in the cell range where you paste.

✔ **Divide** to divide the data you cut or copy to the Clipboard by the data entries in the cell range where you paste.

✔ **Skip Blanks** check box when you want Excel to paste everywhere except for any empty cells in the incoming range. In other words, a blank cell cannot overwrite your current cell entries.

✔ **Transpose** check box when you want Excel to change the orientation of the pasted entries. For example, if the original cells' entries run down the rows of a single column of the worksheet, the transposed pasted entries will run across the columns of a single row.

✔ **Paste Link** button when you're copying cell entries and you want to establish a link between copies you're pasting and the original entries. That way, changes to the original cells automatically update in the pasted copies.

Let's Be Clear about Deleting Stuff

No discussion about editing in Excel would be complete without a section on getting rid of the stuff you put into cells. You can perform two kinds of deletions in a worksheet:

- ✔ **Clearing a cell:** Clearing just deletes or empties the cell's contents without removing the cell from the worksheet, which would alter the layout of the surrounding cells.

- ✔ **Deleting a cell:** Deleting gets rid of the whole kit and caboodle — cell structure along with all its contents and formatting. When you delete a cell, Excel has to shuffle the position of entries in the surrounding cells to plug up any gaps made by the action.

Sounding the all clear!

To get rid of just the contents of a cell selection rather than delete the cells and their contents, select the range of cells to clear and then simply press the Delete key.

If you want to get rid of more than just the contents of a cell selection, click the Clear button (the one with the eraser) in the Editing group on the Ribbon's Home tab and then click one of the following options on its drop-down menu:

- ✔ **Clear All:** Gets rid of all formatting and notes, as well as entries in the cell selection (Alt+HEA).

- ✔ **Clear Formats:** Deletes only the formatting from the cell selection without touching anything else (Alt+HEF).

✔ **Clear Contents:** Deletes only the entries in the cell selection just like pressing the Delete key (Alt+HEC).

✔ **Clear Comments:** Removes the notes in the cell selection but leaves everything else behind (Alt+HEM).

✔ **Clear Hyperlinks:** Removes the active hyperlinks in the cell selection but leaves its descriptive text (Alt+HEL).

Get these cells outta here!

To delete the cell selection rather than just clear out its contents, select the cell range, click the drop-down button attached to the Delete command button in the Cells group of the Home tab, and then click Delete Cells on the drop-down menu (or press Alt+HDD). The Delete dialog box opens, showing options for filling in the gaps created when the cells currently selected are blotted out of existence:

✔ **Shift Cells Left:** This default option moves entries from neighboring columns on the right to the left to fill in gaps created when you delete the cell selection by clicking OK or pressing Enter.

✔ **Shift Cells Up:** Select this option to move entries up from neighboring rows below.

✔ **Entire Row:** Select this option to remove all the rows in the current cell selection.

✔ **Entire Columns:** Select this option to delete all the columns in the current cell selection.

If you know that you want to shift the remaining cells to the left after deleting the cells in the current selection, you can simply click the Delete command button on the Home tab of the

Ribbon. (Taking this action is the same as opening the Delete dialog box and then clicking OK when the default Shift Cells Left button is selected.)

To delete an entire column or row from the worksheet, you can select the column or row on the workbook window frame, right-click the selection, and then click Delete from the column's or row's shortcut menu.

You can also delete entire columns and rows selected in the worksheet by clicking the drop-down button attached to the Delete command button on the Ribbon's Home tab and then clicking the Delete Sheet Columns (Alt+HDC) option or the Delete Sheet Rows option (Alt+HDR) on the drop-down menu.

Deleting entire columns and rows from a worksheet is risky business unless you are sure that the columns and rows in question contain nothing of value. Remember, when you delete an entire row from the worksheet, you delete *all information from column A through XFD* in that row (and you can see only a very few columns in this row). Likewise, when you delete an entire column from the worksheet, you delete *all information from row 1 through 1,048,576* in that column.

Staying in Step with Insert

For those inevitable times when you need to squeeze new entries into an already populated region of the worksheet, you can insert new cells in the area rather than go through all the trouble of moving and rearranging several individual cell ranges. To insert a new cell range, select the cells (many of which are already occupied) where you want the new cells to appear and then click the drop-down attached to the Insert

command button in the Cells group of the Home tab
and then click Insert Cells on the drop-down menu (or
press Alt+HII). The Insert dialog box opens with the
following option buttons:

✔ **Shift Cells Right:** Select this option to shift existing cells to the right to make room for the ones
you want to add before clicking OK or pressing
Enter.

✔ **Shift Cells Down:** Use this default to instruct the
program to shift existing entries down before
clicking OK or pressing Enter.

✔ **Entire Row** or **Entire Column:** When you insert
cells with the Insert dialog box, you can insert
complete rows or columns in the cell range by
selecting either of these radio buttons. You can
also select the row number or column letter on
the frame before you choose the Insert command.

If you know that you want to shift the existing
cells to the right to make room for the newly
inserted cells, you can simply click the Insert
command button on the Ribbon's Home tab
(this is the same thing as opening the Insert
dialog box and then clicking OK when the Shift
Cells Right button is selected).

Remember that you can also insert entire columns and rows in a worksheet by right-clicking
the selection and then clicking Insert on the column's or row's shortcut menu.

As when you delete whole columns and rows,
inserting entire columns and rows affects the
entire worksheet, not just the part you see. If
you don't know what's out in the hinterlands of
the worksheet, you can't be sure how the insertion will affect — perhaps even sabotage — stuff
(especially formulas) in the other unseen areas.

I suggest that you scroll all the way out in both directions to make sure that nothing's out there.

Chapter 4

Formatting a Spreadsheet

. . . .

In This Chapter

▶ Selecting the cells to format

▶ Formatting cell ranges from the Home tab

▶ Working with the Mini-Toolbar

▶ Using number formats on cells containing values

▶ Adjusting column width and row height

▶ Tweaking your fonts

▶ Changing how your cells line up

. . . .

*I*n spreadsheet programs like Excel, you normally don't worry about how the stuff looks until after you enter all the data in the worksheets of your workbook and save it all safe and sound (see Chapters 1 and 2). Only then do you pretty up the information so that it's clearer and easy to read.

After you decide on the types of formatting you want to apply, you select the cells to beautify and click the appropriate tool or choose the menu command to apply those formats to the cells. In this chapter, you delve in to the fabulous formatting features available. First, though, you need to know how to select the group of cells you want to apply the formatting to.

Choosing a Group of Cells

A *cell selection* (or *cell range*) is whatever collection of neighboring cells you choose to format or edit. The smallest possible cell selection in a worksheet is just one cell: the so-called *active cell*. The cell with the cell cursor is really just a single cell selection. The largest possible cell selection in a worksheet is all the cells in that worksheet (the whole enchilada, so to speak). Most of the cell selections you need for formatting a worksheet will probably fall somewhere in between, consisting of cells in several adjacent columns and rows.

Excel shows a cell selection in the worksheet by highlighting in color the entire block of cells within the extended cell cursor except for the active cell that keeps its original color. (Figure 4-1 shows several cell selections of different sizes and shapes.)

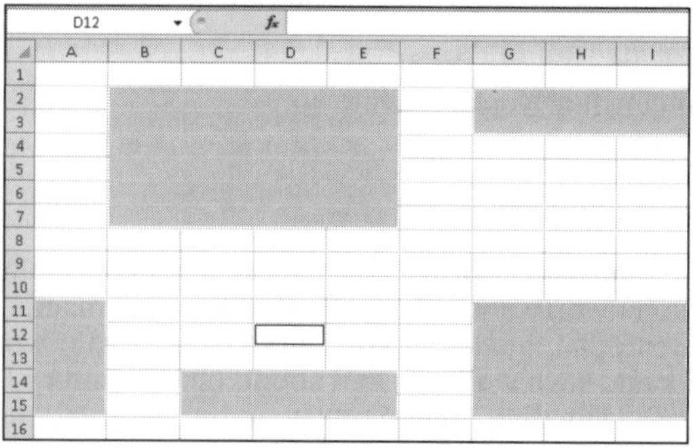

Figure 4-1: Several cell selections of various shapes and sizes.

In Excel, you can select more than one cell range at a time (a phenomenon somewhat ingloriously called a *noncontiguous* or *nonadjacent selection*). In fact, although Figure 4-1 appears to contain several cell selections, it's really just one big, nonadjacent cell selection with cell D12 (the active one) as the cell that was selected last.

Point-and-click cell selections

The mouse is a natural for selecting a range of cells. Just position the mouse pointer (in its thick, white cross form) on the first cell and then click and drag in the direction that you want to extend the selection.

- ✔ To extend the cell selection to columns to the right, drag your mouse to the right, highlighting neighboring cells as you go.
- ✔ To extend the selection to rows to the bottom, drag your mouse down.
- ✔ To extend the selection down and to the right at the same time, drag your mouse diagonally toward the cell in the lower-right corner of the block you're highlighting.

Shifty cell selections

To speed up the old cell-selection procedure, you can use the Shift+click method, which goes as follows:

1. **Click the first cell in the selection to select it.**

2. **Position the mouse pointer in the last cell in the selection.**

   This is kitty-corner from the first cell in your selected rectangular block.

3. **Press the Shift key and hold it down while you click the mouse button again.**

   When you click the mouse button the second time, Excel selects all the cells in the columns and rows between the first cell and last cell.

The Shift key works with the mouse like an *extend* key to extend a selection from the first object you select through to, and including, the second object you select. See the section "Extend that cell selection," later in this chapter. Using the Shift key enables you to select the first and last cells, as well as all the intervening cells in a worksheet or all the document names in a dialog list box.

If, when making a cell selection with the mouse, you notice that you include the wrong cells before you release the mouse button, you can deselect the cells and resize the selection by moving the pointer in the opposite direction. If you already released the mouse button, click the first cell in the highlighted range to select just that cell (and deselect all the others) and then start the whole selection process again.

Nonadjacent cell selections

To select a nonadjacent cell selection made up of more than one non-touching block of cells, drag through the first cell range and release the mouse button. Then hold down the Ctrl key while you click the first cell of the second range and drag the pointer through the cells in this range. As long as you hold down Ctrl while you select the subsequent ranges, Excel doesn't deselect any of the previously selected cell ranges.

The Ctrl key works with the mouse like an *add* key to include non-neighboring objects in Excel. See the section "Nonadjacent cell selections with the keyboard," later in this chapter. By using the Ctrl key, you can add to the selection of cells in a worksheet or to the document names in a dialog list box without having to deselect those already selected.

Going for the "big" cell selections

You can select the cells in entire columns or rows or even all the cells in the worksheet by applying the following clicking-and-dragging techniques to the worksheet frame:

✔ **To select every single cell in a particular column:** Click its column letter on the frame at the top of the worksheet document window.

✔ **To select every cell in a particular row:** Click its row number on the frame at the left edge of the document window.

✔ **To select a range of entire columns or rows:** Drag through the column letters or row numbers on the frame surrounding the workbook.

✔ **To select more than entire columns or rows that are not right next to each other (noncontiguous):** Press and hold down the Ctrl key while you click the column letters or row numbers of the columns and rows that you want to add to the selection.

 To select every cell in the worksheet: Press Ctrl+A or click the Select All button, which is the button with the triangle pointing downward on the diagonal in the upper-left corner of the workbook frame, formed by the intersection of the row with the column letters and the column with the row numbers.

Selecting the cells in a table of data, courtesy of AutoSelect

Excel provides a quick way (called AutoSelect) to select all the cells in a table of data entered as a solid block. To use AutoSelect, simply follow these steps:

1. **Click the first cell of the table to select it.**

   This is the cell in the table's upper-left corner.

2. **Hold down the Shift key while you double-click the right or bottom edge of the selected cell with the arrowhead mouse pointer (see Figure 4-2).**

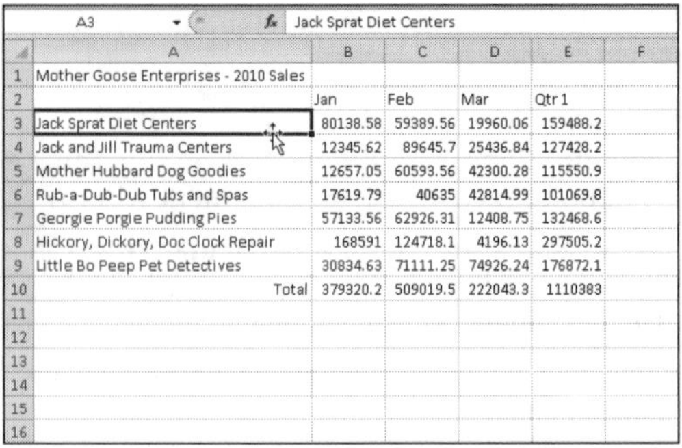

Figure 4-2: Position the mouse pointer on the first cell's bottom edge to select all cells of the table's first column.

Double-clicking the bottom edge of the cell causes the cell selection to expand to the cell in the last row of the first column (as shown in Figure 4-3). If you double-click the right edge of the cell, the cell selection expands to the cell in the last column of the first row.

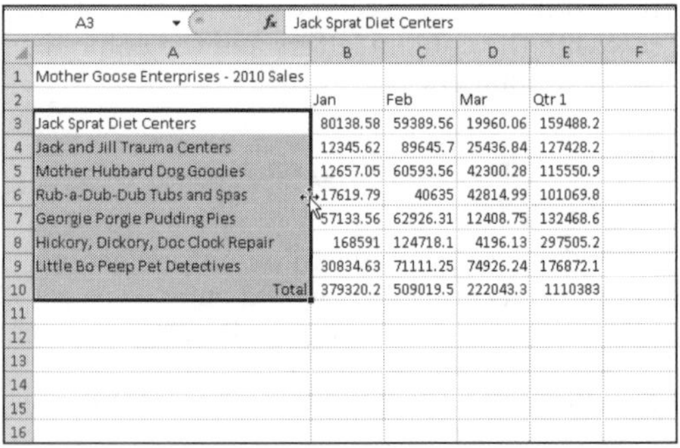

Figure 4-3: Hold down Shift while you double-click the bottom edge of the first cell to extend the selection down the column.

3a. Double-click somewhere on the right edge of the cell selection (refer to Figure 4-3) if the cell selection now consists of the first column of the table.

This selects all the remaining rows of the table of data (as shown in Figure 4-4).

	A	B	C	D	E	F
	A3	▾ (ͫ	*fx*	Jack Sprat Diet Centers		
1	Mother Goose Enterprises - 2010 Sales					
2		Jan	Feb	Mar	Qtr 1	
3	Jack Sprat Diet Centers	80138.58	59389.56	19960.06	159488.2	
4	Jack and Jill Trauma Centers	12345.62	89645.7	25436.84	127428.2	
5	Mother Hubbard Dog Goodies	12657.05	60593.56	42300.28	115550.9	
6	Rub-a-Dub-Dub Tubs and Spas	1765.79	40635	42814.99	101069.8	
7	Georgie Porgie Pudding Pies	57133.56	62926.31	12408.75	132468.6	
8	Hickory, Dickory, Doc Clock Repair	168591	124718.1	4196.13	297505.2	
9	Little Bo Peep Pet Detectives	30834.63	71111.25	74926.24	176872.1	
10	Total	379920.2	509019.5	222043.3	1110383	
11						
12						
13						
14						
15						
16						

Figure 4-4: Hold down Shift and double-click the right edge of the current selection to extend it across the rows of the table.

3b. Double-click somewhere on the bottom edge of the current cell selection if the cell selection now consists of the first row of the table.

This selects all the remaining rows in the table.

Keyboard cell selections

If you're not keen on using the mouse, you can use the keyboard to select the cells you want. Sticking with the Shift+click method of selecting cells, the easiest way to select cells with the keyboard is to combine the Shift key with other keystrokes that move the cell cursor (I list these keystrokes in Chapter 1).

Start by positioning the cell cursor in the first cell of
the selection and then holding the Shift key while you
press the appropriate cell-pointer movement keys.
When you hold the Shift key while you press direction
keys — such as the arrow keys ($\uparrow$, $\rightarrow$, $\downarrow$, $\leftarrow$), PgUp, or
PgDn — Excel anchors the selection on the current
cell, moves the cell cursor, and highlights cells as it
goes.

When making a cell selection this way, you can
continue to alter the size and shape of the cell
range with the cell-pointer movement keys as
long as you don't release the Shift key. After you
release the Shift key, pressing any of the cell-
pointer movement keys immediately collapses
the selection, reducing it to just the cell with the
cell cursor.

Extend that cell selection

If holding the Shift key while you move the cell cursor
is too tiring, you can place Excel in Extend mode by
pressing (and promptly releasing) F8 before you press
any cell-pointer movement key. Excel displays the
Extend Selection indicator on the left side of the Status
bar — when you see this indicator, the program will
select all the cells that you move the cell cursor
through (just as though you were holding down the
Shift key).

After you highlight all the cells you want in the cell
range, press F8 again (or Esc) to turn off Extend mode.
The Extend Selection indicator disappears from the
status bar, and then you can once again move the cell
cursor with the keyboard without highlighting everything in your path. In fact, when you first move the
pointer, all previously selected cells are deselected.

Nonadjacent cell selections with the keyboard

Selecting more than one cell range is a little more complicated with the keyboard than it is with the mouse. When using the keyboard, you alternate between *anchoring* the cell cursor and moving it to select the cell range and *unanchoring* the cell cursor and repositioning it at the beginning of the next range. To unanchor the cell cursor so that you can move it into position for selecting another range, press Shift+F8. This puts you in Add to Selection mode, in which you can move to the first cell of the next range without selecting any more cells. Excel lets you know that the cell cursor is unanchored by displaying the Add to Selection indicator on the left side of the Status bar.

To select more than one cell range by using the keyboard, follow these general steps:

1. **Move the cell cursor to the first cell of the first cell range that you want to select.**

2. **Press F8 to get into Extend Selection mode.**

   Move the cell cursor to select all the cells in the first cell range. Alternatively, hold the Shift key while you move the cell cursor.

3. **Press Shift+F8 to switch from Extend Selection mode to Add to Selection mode.**

   The Add to Selection indicator appears in the Status bar.

4. **Move the cell cursor to the first cell of the next nonadjacent range that you want to select.**

5. **Press F8 again to get back into Extend Selection mode and then move the cell cursor to select all the cells in this new range.**

6. **If you still have other nonadjacent ranges to select, repeat Steps 3, 4, and 5 until you select and add all the cell ranges that you want to use.**

Formatting from the Home Tab

The formatting buttons that appear in the Font, Alignment, and Number groups on the Home tab enable you to target and add formatting to specific cells. Figures 4-5, 4-6, and 4-7 identify all the formatting buttons in these three groups on the Home tab.

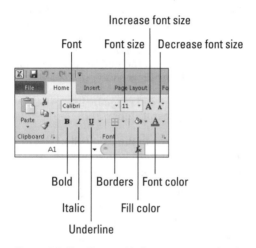

Figure 4-5: The Home tab's Font group contains the tools you commonly need when modifying the appearance of the text in a cell range.

Top align

Middle align

Bottom align

Orientation

Wrap text

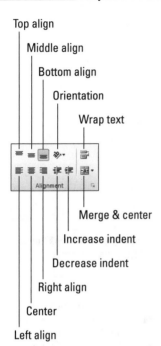

Merge & center

Increase indent

Decrease indent

Right align

Center

Left align

Figure 4-6: The Home tab's Alignment group contains the tools you commonly need when modifying the placement of the text in a cell range.

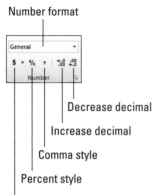

Number format

Decrease decimal

Increase decimal

Comma style

Percent style

Accounting number format

Figure 4-7: The Home tab's Number group contains the tools you commonly need when modifying the number format of the values in a cell range.

Don't forget about these shortcut keys for quickly adding or removing attributes from the entries in the cell selection: Ctrl+B for toggling on and off bold in the cell selection, Ctrl+I for toggling on and off italic, and Ctrl+U for toggling on and off underlining.

Formatting Cells Close to the Source with the Mini-Toolbar

Excel 2010 makes it easy to apply common formatting changes to a cell selection right within the Worksheet area thanks to its new Mini-Toolbar feature, nicknamed the mini-bar (makes me thirsty just thinking about it!).

To display the mini-bar, select the cells that need formatting and then right-click somewhere in the cell selection. The Mini-Toolbar then appears immediately above the cell selection (see Figure 4-8).

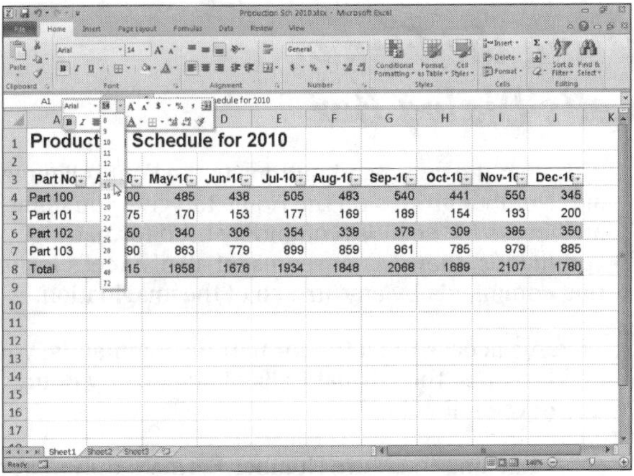

Figure 4-8: Use the buttons on the Mini-Toolbar to apply common formatting changes to the cell selection within the Worksheet area.

As you can see in this figure, the Mini-Toolbar contains most of the buttons from the Font group of the Home tab (with the exception of the Underline button). It also contains the Center and Merge & Center buttons from the Alignment group (see "Altering the Alignment" later in this chapter) and the Accounting Number Format, Percent Style, Comma Style, Increase Decimal, and Decrease Decimal buttons from the Number group (see "Getting comfortable with the number formats" later in this chapter). Simply click these buttons to apply their formatting to the current cell selection.

Additionally, the mini-bar contains the Format Painter button from the Clipboard group of the Home tab that you can use to copy the formatting in the active cell to a cell selection you.

Using the Format Cells Dialog Box

Although the command buttons in the Font, Alignment, and Number groups on the Home tab give you immediate access to the most commonly used formatting commands, they do not represent all of Excel's formatting commands by any stretch of the imagination.

To have access to all the formatting commands, you need to open the Format Cells dialog box by doing any of the following:

- ✔ Clicking the More Number Formats option at the very bottom of the drop-down menu attached to the Number Format button

- ✔ Clicking the dialog box launcher in the lower right of the Number group

- ✔ Pressing Ctrl+1

The Format Cells dialog box that this command calls up contains six tabs: Number, Alignment, Font, Border, Fill, and Protection. In this chapter, I show you how to use the first five tabs.

 The keystroke shortcut that opens the Format Cells dialog box — Ctrl+1 — is one worth knowing. Just press the Ctrl key plus the *number* 1 key, and not the *function key* F1.

Getting comfortable with the number formats

As I explain in Chapter 2, how you enter values into a worksheet determines the type of number format assigned to the values. Here are some examples:

✔ If you enter a financial value complete with the dollar sign and two decimal places, Excel assigns a Currency number format to the cell along with the entry.

✔ If you enter a value representing a percentage as a whole number followed by the percent sign without any decimal places, Excel assigns the cell the Percentage number format that follows this pattern along with the entry.

✔ If you enter a date (dates are values, too) that follows one of the built-in Excel number formats, such as 11/06/02 or 06-Nov-02, the program assigns a Date number format that follows the pattern of the date along with a special value representing the date.

Although you can format values in this manner as you go along (which is necessary in the case of dates), you don't have to do it this way. You can always assign a number format to a group of values before or after you enter them. Formatting numbers after you enter them is often the most efficient way to go because it's just a two-step procedure:

1. **Select all the cells containing the values that need dressing up.**

2. **Select the number format that you want to use from the formatting command buttons on the Home tab or the options available on the Number tab in the Format Cells dialog box.**

Even if you're a really good typist and prefer to enter each value exactly as you want it to appear in the worksheet, you still have to resort to using number formats to make the values that are calculated by formulas match the others you enter. This is because Excel applies a General number format (which the Format Cells dialog box defines: "General format cells have no specific number format.") to all the values it calculates, as well as any you enter that don't exactly follow one of the other Excel number formats. The biggest problem with the General format is that it has the nasty habit of dropping all leading and trailing zeros from the entries. This makes it very hard to line up numbers in a column on their decimal points.

You can view this sad state of affairs in Figure 4-9, which is a sample worksheet with the first-quarter 2010 sales figures for Mother Goose Enterprises before any of the values have been formatted. Notice how the decimal places in the monthly sales figures columns zig and zag and don't align according to decimal place. This is the fault of Excel's General number format; the only cure is to format the values with a uniform number format.

Applying the Accounting number format

Given the financial nature of most worksheets, you probably use the Accounting number format more than any other. Applying this format is easy because you can assign it to the cell selection simply by clicking the Accounting Number Format button on the Home tab.

The Accounting number format adds a dollar sign, commas between thousands of dollars, and two decimal places to any values in a selected range. If any of the values in the cell selection are negative, this number format displays them in parentheses (the way accountants like them). If you want a minus sign in front of your negative financial values rather than enclosing them in parentheses, select the Currency format on the Number Format drop-down menu or on the Number tab of the Format Cells dialog box.

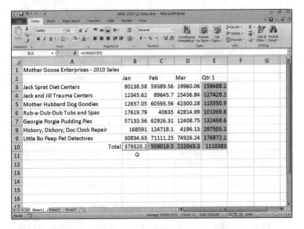

Figure 4-9: Numbers with decimals don't align when you choose General formatting.

You can see in Figure 4-10 only the cells containing totals are selected (cell ranges E3:E10 and B10:D10). This cell selection was then formatted with the Accounting number format by simply clicking its command button (the one with the $ icon) in the Number group on the Home tab.

Although you could put all the figures in the table into the Accounting number format to line up the decimal points, this would result in a superabundance of dollar signs in a fairly small table. In this example, I only formatted the monthly and quarterly totals with the Accounting number format.

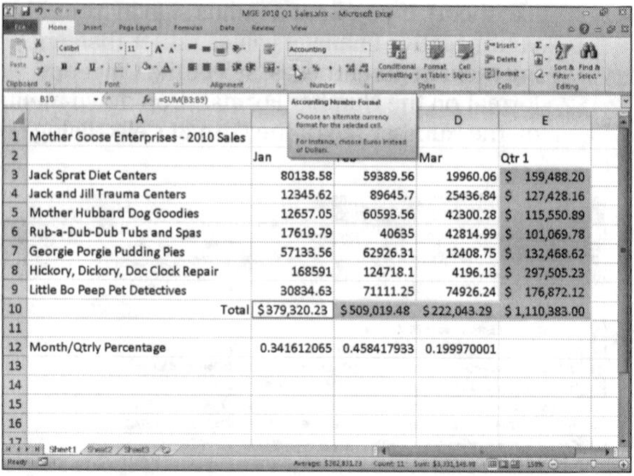

Figure 4-10: The totals in the Mother Goose sales table after clicking the Accounting Number Format button.

"Look, Ma, no more format overflow!"

When I apply the Accounting number format to the selection in the cell ranges of E3:E10 and B10:D10 in the sales table shown in Figure 4-11, Excel adds dollar signs, commas between the thousands, a decimal point, and two decimal places to the highlighted values. At the same time, Excel automatically widens columns B, C, D, and E just enough to display all this new formatting. In versions of Excel earlier than Excel 2003, you had to widen these columns yourself, and instead of the perfectly aligned numbers, you were confronted with columns of #######s in cell ranges E3:E10 and B10:D10. Such pound signs (where nicely formatted dollar totals should be) serve as overflow indicators, declaring that whatever formatting you added to the value in that cell has added so much to the value's display that Excel can no longer display it within the current column width.

Fortunately, Excel eliminates the format overflow indicators when you're formatting the values in your cells by
automatically widening the columns. The only time
you'll ever run across these dreaded #######s in your
cells is when you take it upon yourself to narrow a worksheet column manually (see the section "Calibrating
Columns," later in this chapter) to the extent that Excel
can no longer display all the characters in its cells with
formatted values.

Getting decimals in line by using the Comma Style

The Comma Style format offers a good alternative to
the Currency format. Like Currency, the Comma Style
format inserts commas in larger numbers to separate
thousands, hundred thousands, millions, and . . . well,
you get the idea.

This format also displays two decimal places and puts
negative values in parentheses. What the Comma
Style format doesn't display is dollar signs. So this
format is perfect for formatting tables where it's
obvious that you're dealing with dollars and cents or
for larger values that have nothing to do with money.

The Comma Style format also works well for the bulk of
the values in the sample first-quarter sales worksheet.
Check out Figure 4-11 to see this table after I format the
cells containing the monthly sales for all the Mother
Goose Enterprises with the Comma Style format. To do
this, select the cell range B3:D9 and click the Comma
Style button — the one with the comma icon (,) — in
the Number group on the Home tab.

Note how, in Figure 4-11, the Comma Style format
takes care of the earlier decimal alignment problem in
the quarterly sales figures. Moreover, Comma Style–
formatted monthly sales figures align perfectly with
the Currency format–styled monthly totals in row 10.
If you look closely (you may need a magnifying glass
for this one), you see that these formatted values no

longer abut the right edges of their cells; they've moved slightly to the left. The gap on the right between the last digit and the cell border accommodates the right parenthesis in negative values, ensuring that they, too, align precisely on the decimal point.

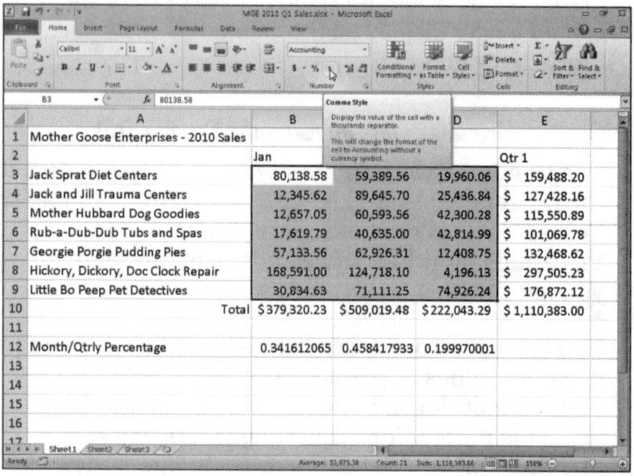

Figure 4-11: Monthly sales figures after formatting cells with the Comma Style number format.

Playing around with Percent Style

Many worksheets use percentages in the form of interest rates, growth rates, inflation rates, and so on. To insert a percentage in a cell, type the percent sign (%) after the number. To indicate an interest rate of 12 percent, for example, you enter **12%** in the cell. Excel assigns a Percentage number format and, at the same time, divides the value by 100 (that's what makes it a percentage) and places the result in the cell (0.12 in this example).

Not all percentages in a worksheet are entered by hand in this manner. Some may be calculated by a formula and returned to their cells as raw decimal values. In such cases, you should add a Percent format to convert the calculated decimal values to percentages (done by multiplying the decimal value by 100 and adding a percent sign).

Deciding how many decimal places

You can increase or decrease the number of decimal places used in a number entered by using the Accounting Number Format, Comma Style, or Percent Style button in the Number group of the Home tab simply by clicking the Increase Decimal button or the Decrease Decimal button in this group.

Each time you click the Increase Decimal button (the one with the arrow pointing left), Excel adds another decimal place to the number format you apply.

The values behind the formatting

Make no mistake about it — all that these fancy number formats do is spiff up the presentation of the values in the worksheet. Like a good illusionist, a particular number format may appear to transform some entries; but in reality, the entries are the same old numbers you started with. For example, suppose that a formula returns the following value:

```
25.6456
```

Now suppose that you format the cell containing this value with the Accounting Number Format button on the Home tab. The value now appears as follows:

```
$25.65
```

This change may lead you to believe that Excel rounded the value up to two decimal places. In fact, the program has rounded up only the *display* of the calculated value — the cell still contains the same old value of 25.6456. If you use this cell in another worksheet formula, Excel uses the behind-the-scenes value in its calculation, not the spiffed-up one shown in the cell.

Ogling some other number formats

Excel supports number formats besides the Accounting, Comma Style, and Percentage number formats. To use them, select the cell range (or ranges) you want to format and select Format Cells on the cell shortcut menu (right-click somewhere in the cell selection to activate this menu) or just press Ctrl+1 to open the Format Cells dialog box.

After the Format Cells dialog box opens with the Number tab displayed, you select the desired format from the Category list box. Some number formats — such as Date, Time, Fraction, and Special — give you further formatting choices in a Type list box. Other number formats, such as Number and Currency, have their own particular boxes that give you options for refining their formats. When you click the different formats in these list boxes, Excel shows what effect this would have on the first of the values in the current cell selection in the Sample area above. When the sample has the format that you want to apply to the current cell selection, you just click OK or press Enter to apply the new number format.

Excel contains a nifty category of number formats called Special. The Special category contains the following four number formats that may interest you:

✔ **Zip Code:** Retains any leading zeros in the value (important for zip codes and of no importance in arithmetic computations). Example: 00123.

✔ **Zip Code + 4:** Automatically separates the last four digits from the first five digits and retains any leading zeros. Example: 00123-5555.

✔ **Phone Number:** Automatically encloses the first three digits of the number in parentheses and separates the last four digits from the previous three with a dash. Example: (999) 555-1111.

✔ **Social Security Number:** Automatically puts dashes in the value to separate its digits into groups of three, two, and four. Example: 666-00-9999.

These Special number formats really come in handy when creating data lists in Excel that often deal with stuff like zip codes, telephone numbers, and sometimes even Social Security numbers.

Calibrating Columns

For those times when Excel 2010 doesn't automatically adjust the width of your columns to your complete satisfaction, the program makes your changing the column widths a breeze. The easiest way to adjust a column is to do a *best-fit,* using the AutoFit feature. With this method, Excel automatically determines how much to widen or narrow the column to fit the longest entry currently in the column.

Here's how to use AutoFit to get the best fit for a column:

1. **Position the mouse pointer on the right border of the worksheet frame with the column letter at the top of the worksheet.**

The mouse pointer changes to a double-headed arrow pointing left and right.

2. Double-click the mouse button.

Excel widens or narrows the column width to suit the longest entry.

You can apply a best-fit to more than one column at a time. Simply select all the columns that need adjusting (if the columns neighbor one another, drag through their column letters on the frame; if they don't, hold down the Ctrl key while you click the individual column letters). After you select the columns, double-click any of the right borders on the frame.

Best-fit à la AutoFit doesn't always produce the expected results. A long title that spills into several columns to the right produces a very wide column when you use best-fit.

When AutoFit's best-fit won't do, drag the right border of the column (on the frame) until it's the size you need instead of double-clicking it. This manual technique for calibrating the column width also works when more than one column is selected. Just be aware that all selected columns assume whatever size you make the one that you're actually dragging.

You can also set the widths of columns from the Format button's drop-down list in the Cells group on the Home tab. When you click this drop-down button, the Cell Size section of this drop-down menu contains the following width options:

✔ **Column Width** to open the Column Width dialog box where you enter the number of characters that you want for the column width before you click OK

  ✔ **AutoFit Column Width** to have Excel apply
    best-fit to the columns based on the widest
    entries in the current cell selection

  ✔ **Default Width** to open the Standard Width
    dialog box containing the standard column
    width of 8.43 characters that you can apply to
    the columns in the cell selection

Rambling Rows

The story with adjusting the heights of rows is pretty
much the same as that with adjusting columns except
that you do a lot less row adjusting than you do column
adjusting. That's because Excel automatically changes
the height of the rows to accommodate changes to their
entries, such as selecting a larger font size or wrapping
text in a cell. I discuss both of these techniques in the
upcoming section "Altering the Alignment." Most row-
height adjustments come about when you want to
increase the amount of space between a table title and
the table or between a row of column headings and the
table of information without actually adding a blank
row. (See the section "From top to bottom," later in this
chapter, for details.)

To increase the height of a row, drag the bottom
border of the row frame down until the row is high
enough and then release the mouse button. To
shorten a row, reverse this process and drag the
bottom row-frame border up. To use AutoFit to best-
fit the entries in a row, you double-click the bottom
row-frame border.

As with columns, you can also adjust the height of
selected rows using row options in the Cell Size section on the Format button's drop-down menu on the
Home tab:

✔ **Row Height** to open the Row Height dialog box where you enter the number of points in the Row Height text box and then click OK

✔ **AutoFit Row Height** to return the height of selected rows to the best fit

Futzing with Fonts

When you start a new worksheet, Excel 2010 assigns a uniform font and type size to all the cell entries you make. The default font varies according to the version of Windows under which you're running Excel. When you run Excel on Windows 7 and Vista, Excel uses its Calibri font (the so-called Body Font) in 11-point size. Although this font may be fine for normal entries, you may want to use something with a little more zing for titles and headings in the worksheet.

Using the buttons in the Font group on the Home tab, you can make most font changes (including selecting a new font style or new font size) without having to resort to changing the settings on the Font tab in the Format Cells dialog box (Ctrl+1):

✔ To select a new font for a cell selection, click the drop-down button next to the Font combo box and then select the name of the font you want to use from the list box. Excel displays the name of each font that appears in this list box in the actual font named (so that the font name becomes an example of what the font looks like — onscreen anyway).

✔ To change the font size, click the drop-down button next to the Font Size combo box, select the new font size or click the Font Size text box, type the new size, and then press Enter.

You can also add the attributes of **bold**, *italic*, <u>underlining</u>, or `strikethrough` to the font you use. The Font group of the Home tab contains the Bold, Italic, and Underline buttons, which not only add these attributes to a cell selection but remove them as well. After you click any of these attribute tools, notice that the tool becomes shaded whenever you position the cell cursor in the cell or cells that contain that attribute. When you click a selected format button to remove an attribute, Excel no longer shades the attribute button when you select the cell.

Although you'll probably make most font changes with the Home tab on the Ribbon, on rare occasions you may find it more convenient to make these changes from the Font tab in the Format Cells dialog box (Ctrl+1).

As you can see in Figure 4-12, this Font tab in the Format Cells dialog box brings together under one roof fonts, font styles (bold and italics), effects (strikethrough, superscript, and subscript), and color changes. When you want to make many font-related changes to a cell selection, working in the Font tab may be your best bet. One of the nice things about using this tab is that it contains a Preview box that shows you how your font changes appear (onscreen at least).

To change the color of the entries in a cell selection, click the Font Color button's drop-down menu in the Font group on the Home tab and then select the color you want the text to appear in the drop-down palette. You can use Live Preview to see what the entries in the cell selection look like in a particular font color by moving the mouse pointer over the color swatches in the palette before you select one by clicking it (assuming, of course, that the palette doesn't cover the cells).

Figure 4-12: Use the Font tab on the Format Cells dialog box to make many font changes at one time.

If you change font colors and then print the worksheet with a black-and-white printer, Excel renders the colors as shades of gray. The Automatic option at the top of the Font Color button's drop-down menu picks up the color assigned in Windows as the window text color. This color is black unless you change it in your display properties.

Altering the Alignment

The horizontal alignment assigned to cell entries when you first make them is simply a function of the type of entry it is: All text entries are left-aligned, and all values are right-aligned with the borders of their cells. However, you can alter this standard arrangement anytime it suits you.

The Alignment group of the Home tab contains three normal horizontal alignment tools: the Align Left, Center, and Align Right buttons. These buttons align the current cell selection exactly as you expect them to. On the right side of the Alignment group, you usually find the special alignment button called Merge & Center.

Despite its rather strange name, you'll want to get to know this button. You can use it to center a worksheet title across the entire width of a table in seconds (or faster, depending upon your machine). I show you in Figures 4-13 and 4-14 how you can use this tool. In Figure 4-13, notice that the worksheet title Mother Goose Enterprises – 2010 Sales is in cell A1. To center this title over the table (which extends from column A through E), select the cell range A1:E1 (the width of the table) and then click the Merge & Center button in the Alignment group on the Ribbon's Home tab.

	A	B	C	D	E
1	Mother Goose Enterprises - 2010 Sales				
2		Jan	Feb	Mar	Qtr 1
3	Jack Sprat Diet Centers	80,138.58	59,389.56	19,960.06	$ 159,488.20
4	Jack and Jill Trauma Centers	12,345.62	89,645.70	25,436.84	$ 127,428.16
5	Mother Hubbard Dog Goodies	12,657.05	60,593.56	42,300.28	$ 115,550.89
6	Rub-a-Dub-Dub Tubs and Spas	17,619.79	40,635.00	42,814.99	$ 101,069.78
7	Georgie Porgie Pudding Pies	57,133.56	62,926.31	12,408.75	$ 132,468.62
8	Hickory, Dickory, Doc Clock Repair	168,591.00	124,718.10	4,196.13	$ 297,505.23
9	Little Bo Peep Pet Detectives	30,834.63	71,111.25	74,926.24	$ 176,872.12
10	Total	$379,320.23	$509,019.48	$222,043.29	$1,110,383.00
11					
12	Month/Qtrly Percentage	34.16%	45.84%	20.00%	
13					
14					
15					
16					

Figure 4-13: A worksheet title before merging and centering.

Look at Figure 4-14 to see the result: The cells in row 1 of columns A through E are merged into one cell, and now the title is properly centered in this "super" cell and consequently over the entire table.

 If you ever need to split up a supercell that you've merged with Merge & Center back into its original, individual cell or cells, select the cell and then simply click the Merge & Center button again.

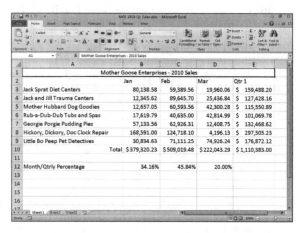

Figure 4-14: A worksheet title after merging and centering it across columns A through E.

Intent on indents

In Excel 2010, you can indent the entries in a cell selection by clicking the Increase Indent button. The Increase Indent button in the Alignment group of the Home tab sports a picture of an arrow pushing the lines of text to the right. Each time you click this button, Excel indents the entries in the current cell selection to the right by three character widths of the standard font. (See the section "Futzing with the Fonts," earlier in this chapter, if you don't know what a standard font is or how to change it.)

You can remove an indent by clicking the Decrease Indent button (to the immediate left of the Increase Indent button) on the Home tab with the picture of the arrow pushing the lines of text to the left. Additionally, you can change how many characters an entry indents with the Increase Indent button (or outdents with the Decrease Indent button). Open the Format Cells dialog box (Ctrl+1). Select the Alignment tab, and then alter the value in the Indent text box (by typing a new value in this text box or by dialing up a new value with its spinner buttons).

From top to bottom

Left, right, and *center* alignment all refer to the horizontal positioning of a text entry in relation to the left and right cell borders (that is, horizontally). You can also align entries in relation to the top and bottom borders of their cells (that is, vertically). Normally, all entries align vertically with the bottom of the cells (as though they were resting on the very bottom of the cell). You can also vertically center an entry in its cell or align it with the top of its cell.

To change the vertical alignment of a cell range that you've selected, click the appropriate button (Top Align, Middle Align, or Bottom Align) in the Alignment group on the Home tab.

Tampering with how the text wraps

Traditionally, column headings in worksheet tables have been a problem — you had to keep them really short or abbreviate them if you wanted to avoid widening all the columns more than the data warranted. You can avoid this problem in Excel by using the Wrap Text button in the Alignment group on the Home tab (the one to the immediate right of the Orientation button). In Figure 4-15, I show a new worksheet in which the column headings containing the various companies within the vast Mother Goose Enterprises conglomerate use the Wrap Text feature to avoid widening the columns as much as these long company names would otherwise require.

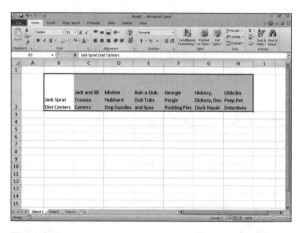

Figure 4-15: A new worksheet with the column headings formatted with the Wrap Text option.

To create the effect shown in Figure 4-15, select the cells with the column headings (the cell range B2:H2) and then click the Wrap Text button in the Alignment group on the Home tab.

Selecting Wrap Text breaks up the long text entries (that either spill over or cut off) in the selection into separate lines. To accommodate more than one line in a cell, the program automatically expands the row height so that the entire wrapped-text entry is visible.

When you select Wrap Text, Excel continues to use the horizontal and vertical alignment you specify for the cell. You can use any of the Horizontal alignment options found on the Alignment tab of the Format Cells dialog box (Ctrl+1), including Left (Indent), Center, Right (Indent), Justify, or Center Across Selection. However, you can't use the Fill option or Distributed (Indent) option. Select the Fill option on the Horizontal drop-down list box only when you want Excel to repeat the entry across the entire width of the cell.

If you want to wrap a text entry in its cell and have Excel justify the text with both the left and right borders of the cell, select the Justify option from the Horizontal drop-down list box in the Alignment tab in the Format Cells dialog box.

 You can break a long text entry into separate lines by positioning the insertion point in the cell entry (or on the Formula bar) at the place where you want the new line to start and pressing Alt+Enter. Excel expands the row containing the cell (and the Formula bar above) when it starts a new line. When you press Enter to complete the entry or edit, Excel automatically wraps the text in the cell, according to the cell's column width and the position of the line break.

Shrink to fit

For those times when you need to prevent Excel from widening the column to fit its cell entries (as may be the case when you need to display an entire table of data on a single screen or printed page), use the Shrink to Fit text control.

Click the Alignment tab of the Format Cells dialog box (Ctrl+1) and then click the Shrink to Fit check box in the Text Control section. Excel reduces the font size of the entries to the selected cells so that they don't require changing the current column width. Just be aware when using this Text Control option that, depending on the length of the entries and width of the column, you can end up with some text entries so small that they're completely illegible!

Bring on the borders!

The gridlines you normally see in the worksheet to separate the columns and rows are just guidelines to help you keep your place as you build your spreadsheet. You can choose to print them with your data or not (by checking or clearing the Print check box that appears in the Gridlines section of the Sheet Options group on the Page Layout tab).

To emphasize sections of the worksheet or parts of a particular table, you can add borderlines or shading to certain cells. Don't confuse the *borderlines* that you add to accent a particular cell selection with the *gridlines* used to define cell borders in the worksheet — borders that you add print regardless of whether you print the worksheet gridlines.

 To see the borders that you add to the cells in a worksheet, remove the gridlines normally displayed in the worksheet by clearing the View check box in the Gridlines section of the Sheet Options group on the Page Layout tab.

To add borders to a cell selection, click the drop-down button attached to the Borders button in the Font group on the Home tab. This displays a drop-down menu with all the border options you can apply to the cell selection (see Figure 4-16) where you click the type of line you want to apply to all its cells.

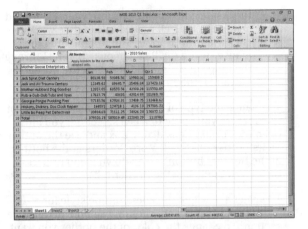

Figure 4-16: Select borders for a cell selection with the Borders button on the Home tab.

When selecting options on this drop-down menu to determine where you want the borderlines drawn, keep these things in mind:

- ✔ To have Excel draw borders only around the outside edges of the entire cell selection (in other words, following the path of the expanded cell cursor), click the Outside Borders or the Thick Box Border options on this menu. To draw the outside borders yourself around an unselected cell range in the active worksheet, click the Draw Border option, drag the mouse (using the Pencil mouse pointer) through the range of cells, and then click the Borders button on the Home tab's Font group.

- ✔ If you want borderlines to appear around all four edges of each cell in the cell selection (like a paned window), select the All Borders option on this drop-down menu. If you want to draw the inside and outside borders yourself around an unselected cell range in the active worksheet, click the Draw Border Grid option, drag the mouse (using the Pencil mouse pointer) through the range of cells, and then click the Borders button on the Home tab.

To change the type of line, line thickness, or color of the borders you apply to a cell selection, you must open the Format Cells dialog box and use the options on its Border tab (click More Borders at the bottom of the Borders button's drop-down menu or press Ctrl+1 and then click the Border tab).

To select a new line thickness or line style for a border you're applying, click its example in the Style section. To change the color of the border you want to apply, click the color sample on the Color drop-down palette. After you select a new line style and/or color, apply the border to the cell selection by click-ing the appropriate line in either the Presets or Border section of the Border tab before you click OK.

To get rid of existing borders in a worksheet, you must select the cell or cells that presently contain them and then click the No Border option at the top of the second section on the Borders button's drop-down menu.

Applying fill colors, patterns, and gradient effects to cells

You can also add emphasis to particular sections of the worksheet or one of its tables by changing the fill color of the cell selection and/or applying a pattern or gradient to it.

If you're using a black-and-white printer, you want to restrict your color choices to light gray in the color palette. Additionally, you want to

> restrict your use of pattern styles to the very
> open ones with few dots when enhancing a cell
> selection that contains any kind of entries (oth-
> erwise, the entries will be almost impossible to
> read when printed).

To choose a new fill color for the background of a cell
selection, you can click the Fill Color button's drop-
down menu in the Font group on the Home tab and
then select the color you want to use in the drop-
down palette. Remember that you can use Live
Preview to see what the cell selection looks like in a
particular fill color by moving the mouse pointer over
the color swatches. Click one to select it.

To choose a new pattern for a cell selection, you must
open the Format Cells dialog box (Ctrl+1), and then
click the Fill tab. To change the pattern of the cell
selection, click a pattern swatch from the Pattern
Style button's pattern palette. To add a fill color to
the pattern you select, click its color swatch in the
Background Color section of the Fill tab.

If you want to add a gradient effect to the cell selection that goes from one color to another in a certain
direction, click the Fill Effects button on the Fill tab to
open the Fill Effects dialog box (see Figure 4-17). This
dialog box contains a Gradient tab with controls that
enable you to determine the two colors to use as well
as shading style and variant.

After you select the colors and styles of the gradient,
check the Sample swatch in the Fill Effects dialog box.
When you have it the way you want it, click OK to
close the Fill Effects dialog box and return to the
Format Cells dialog box. The selected gradient effect
then appears in its Sample area on the Fill tab in the
Format Cells dialog box. Unfortunately, this is one
area where Live Preview doesn't work, so you're just
going to have to click its OK button to apply the

gradient to the cell selection to see how it actually looks in the worksheet.

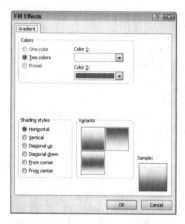

Figure 4-17: Select a new gradient for a cell selection in the Fill Effects dialog box.

Although you can't select new patterns or gradients (only colors) with the Fill Color button on the Home tab, you can remove fill colors, patterns, and gradients assigned to a cell selection by clicking the No Fill option on the Fill Color button's drop-down menu.

Chapter 5

Printing a Spreadsheet

. . . .

In This Chapter

▶ Previewing pages in Page Layout View and printouts in Backstage View

▶ Quick Printing from the Quick Access toolbar

▶ Changing page orientation

▶ Printing the whole worksheet on a single page

▶ Changing margins

▶ Adding a header and footer

▶ Printing column and row headings as print titles

▶ Fixing page breaks

▶ Printing formulas

. . . .

*F*or most people, getting data down on paper is what spreadsheets are all about. All the data entry, all the formatting, all the formula checking, and all the other things you do to get a spreadsheet ready is really just preparation for printing its information.

In this chapter, you find out how easy it is to print reports with Excel 2010. The only trick to printing a worksheet is learning how to control the paging scheme. Many of the worksheets you create with Excel are not only longer than one printed page but also wider. Spreadsheet programs like Excel 2010 often have to break up pages both vertically and horizontally to print a worksheet document.

When breaking a worksheet into pages, Excel first pages the document vertically down the rows in the first columns of the print area. After paging the first columns, the program pages down the rows of the second set of columns in the print area. Excel pages down and then over until the entire document included in the current print area (which can include the entire worksheet or just sections) is paged.

When paging the worksheet, Excel doesn't break up the information within a row or column. If not all the information in a row will fit at the bottom of the page, the program moves the entire row to the following page. If not all the information in a column will fit at the right edge of the page, the program moves the entire column to a new page. Because Excel pages down and then over, the column may not appear on the next page of the report.

In this chapter, you see all the ways in which you can deal with such paging problems.

Taking a Gander at the Pages in Page Layout View

Excel 2010's Page Layout View gives you instant access to the paging of the current worksheet. Activate this feature by clicking the Page Layout View button (the center one) to the immediate left of the Zoom slider on the Status bar or by clicking the Page Layout View command button on the Ribbon's View tab (Alt+WP). As you can see in Figure 5-1, when you switch to Page Layout View, Excel adds horizontal and vertical rulers to the column letter and row number headings. In the Worksheet area, this view

shows the margins for each printed page, any headers
and footers defined for the report, and the breaks
between each page. (Often, you have to use the Zoom
slider to reduce the screen magnification to display
the page breaks on the screen.)

Excel displays rulers using the default units for
your computer (inches on a U.S. computer and
centimeters on a European machine). To change
the units, open the Advanced tab of the Excel
Options dialog box (File➪Options➪Advanced or
Alt+FIA) and then select the appropriate unit
(Inches, Centimeters, or Millimeters) on the Ruler
Units drop-down menu in the Display section.

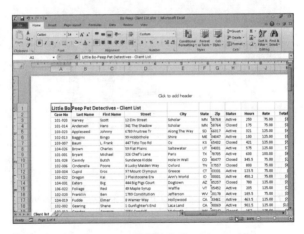

Figure 5-1: Viewing a spreadsheet in Page Layout View.

The Ruler check box on the View tab acts as a
toggle switch. The first time you click this
button, Excel removes the rulers from the Page
Layout View; click again, and the program adds
them back.

Checking and Printing a Report from the Print Panel

To save paper and your sanity, print your worksheet directly from the Print panel in Backstage View by clicking File⇨Print (or simply pressing Ctrl+P or Ctrl+F2). As you see in Figure 5-2, the Print panel shows your current print settings, along with a preview of the first page.

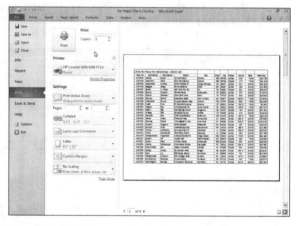

Figure 5-2: The Print panel in Backstage View shows your current print settings plus a preview of the printout.

You can use the Print Preview feature in the Print panel before you print any worksheet, section of worksheet, or entire workbook. Because of the peculiarities in how worksheet data is paged, you often need to check the page breaks for any report that requires more than one page. The print preview area in the Print panel shows you exactly how the worksheet data will page when printed. If necessary, you can return to the worksheet where you can make changes to the page settings from the Page Layout tab on the Ribbon before sending the report to the printer when everything looks okay.

When Excel displays a full page in the print preview area, you can barely read its contents. To increase the view to actual size to verify some of the data, click the Zoom to Page button in the lower-right corner of the Print panel. Check out the difference in Figure 5-3. You can see what the first page of the four-page report looks like after I zoom in by clicking the Zoom to Page button.

After you enlarge a page to actual size, use the scroll bars to bring new parts of the page into view in the print preview area. To return to the full-page view, click the Zoom to Page button a second time to deselect it.

Excel indicates the number of pages in a report at the bottom of the print preview area. If your report has more than one page, you can view pages that follow by clicking the Next Page button to the right of the final page number. To review a page you've already seen, back up a page by clicking the Previous Page button to the left of the first page number. (The Previous Page button is gray if you're on the first page.)

To display markers indicating the current left, right, top, and bottom margins along with the column widths, select the Show Margins check box to the immediate left of the Zoom to Page button. You can then modify the column widths as well as the page margins by dragging the appropriate marker.

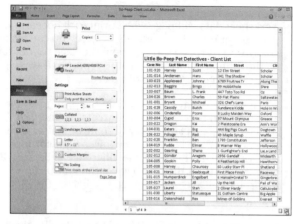

Figure 5-3: Page 1 of a four-page report after clicking the Zoom to Page button.

When you finish previewing the report, the Print panel offers you the following options for changing certain print settings before you send it to the printer:

✔ **Print button with the Number of Copies combo box:** Use this button to print the spreadsheet report using the current print settings listed on the panel. Use the combo box to indicate the number of copies you want when you need multiple copies printed.

✔ **Printer drop-down button:** Use this button to select a new printer or fax to send the spreadsheet report to when more than one device is installed. (Excel automatically displays the name of the printer that's installed as the default printer in Windows.)

✔ **Print What drop-down button and attendant Pages combo boxes:** Use the Print What drop-down button to choose between printing only the active (selected) worksheets in the workbook (the default), the entire workbook, the current cell selection in the current worksheet, and the currently selected table in the current worksheet. Use the combo boxes to restrict what's printed to just the range of pages you enter in these boxes or select with their spinner buttons.

Beneath the combo boxes, you find drop-down list buttons to print on both sides of each page in the report, collate the pages of the report, and switch the page orientation from Portrait (aligned with the short side) to Landscape (aligned with the long side). Additionally, you can select a paper size other than the standard 8.5" x 11" letter, and customize the size of the report's margins (top, bottom, left, and right, as well as the margins for any header and footer on the page).

Printing the Current Worksheet

If you're using Excel's default print settings to print all the cells in the current worksheet, printing in Excel 2010 is a breeze. Simply add the Quick Print button to the Quick Access toolbar (by clicking the Customize Quick Access Toolbar button and then clicking Quick Print on its drop-down menu) and then click this button to print a single copy of all the information in the current worksheet, including any charts and graphics — but not including comments you add to cells.

While Excel sends the print job to the print queue, Excel displays a Printing dialog box to inform you of its progress (displaying such updates as *Printing Page 2 of 3*). After this dialog box disappears, you are free to go back to work in Excel. To stop printing while the job is still being sent to the print queue, click the Cancel button in the Printing dialog box.

If you don't realize that you want to cancel the print job until after Excel finishes shipping it to the print queue (that is, while the Printing dialog box appears onscreen), you must:

1. **Click the printer icon in the Notification area at the far right of the Windows taskbar (to the immediate left of the current time) with the secondary mouse button to open its shortcut menu.**

   This printer icon displays the ScreenTip *1 document(s) pending for so-and-so* when you position the mouse pointer over the printer icon.

2. **Right-click the printer icon and select Open All Active Printers from the shortcut menu.**

   This opens the dialog box for the printer with the Excel print job in its queue (as described under the Document Name heading in the list box).

3. **Select the Excel print job that you want to cancel in the list box of your printer's dialog box.**

4. **Choose Document↪Cancel from the menu bar and then click Yes to confirm you want to cancel the print job.**

5. **Wait for the print job to disappear from the queue in the printer's dialog box and then click Close.**

My Page Was Set Up!

About the only thing the slightest bit complex in printing a worksheet is figuring out how to get the pages right. Fortunately, the command buttons in the Page Setup group on the Ribbon's Page Layout tab give you a great deal of control over what goes on which page.

Three groups of buttons on the Page Layout tab help
you get your page settings exactly as you want them.
The Page Setup group, the Scale to Fit group, and the
Sheet Options group are described in the following
sections.

 To see the effect of changes you make in the
Worksheet area, put the worksheet into Page
Layout View by clicking the Page Layout button
on the Status bar while you work with the
command buttons in the Page Setup, Scale to
Fit, and Sheet Options groups on the Page
Layout tab of the Ribbon.

Using the Page Setup buttons

The Page Setup group of the Page Layout tab contains
the following important command buttons:

✔ **Margins:** Select one of three preset margins for
the report or set custom margins on the Margins
tab of the Page Setup dialog box. (See "Massaging
the margins" that follows in this chapter.)

✔ **Orientation:** Switch between Portrait and
Landscape mode for printing. (See the "Getting
the lay of the landscape" section, later in this
chapter.)

✔ **Size:** Select one of the preset paper sizes, set a
custom size, or change the printing resolution
or page number on the Page tab of the Page
Setup dialog box.

✔ **Print Area:** Set and clear the print area.

✔ **Breaks:** Insert or remove page breaks. (See
"Solving Page Break Problems" later in this
chapter.)

✔ **Background:** Open the Sheet Background dialog box where you can select a new graphic image or photo to use as a background for the current worksheet. (This button changes to Delete Background when you select a background image.)

✔ **Print Titles:** Open the Sheet tab of the Page Setup dialog box where you can define rows to repeat at the top and columns to repeat at the left as *titles* for the report. (See "Putting out the print titles" later in this chapter.)

Massaging the margins

The Normal margin settings that Excel applies to a new report uses standard top, bottom, left, and right margins of ¾ inch with just over a ¼ inch separating the header and footer from the top and bottom margins, respectively.

In addition to the Normal margin settings, the program enables you to select two other standard margins from the Margins button's drop-down menu:

✔ **Wide:** Provides 1-inch top, bottom, left, and right margins and ½ inch separating the header and footer from the top and bottom margins, respectively.

✔ **Narrow:** Provides a top and bottom margin of ¾ inch and a left and right margin of ¼ inch with 0.3 inch separating the header and footer from the top and bottom margins, respectively.

Frequently, you find yourself with a report that takes up a full printed page and then just enough to spill over onto a second, mostly empty, page. To squeeze the last column or the last few rows of the worksheet data onto Page 1, try selecting Narrow on the Margins button's drop-down menu.

If that doesn't do it, you can try manually adjusting the margins for the report from the Margins tab of the Page Setup dialog box or by dragging the margin markers in the preview area of the Print panel in the Backstage View (Press Ctrl+P and click the Show Margins button). To get more columns on a page, try reducing the left and right margins. To get more rows on a page, try reducing the top and bottom margins.

To open the Margins tab of the Page Setup dialog box (shown in Figure 5-4), click Custom Margins on the Margins button's drop-down menu. There, enter the new settings in the Top, Bottom, Left, and Right text boxes — or select the new margin settings with their respective spinner buttons.

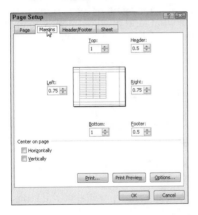

Figure 5-4: Adjust your report margins from the Margins tab in the Page Setup dialog box.

 Select one or both Center on Page options in the Margins tab of the Page Setup dialog box (refer to Figure 5-4) to center a selection of data (that takes up less than a full page) between the current margin settings. In the Center on Page section, select the Horizontally check box to center the data between the left and right margins. Select the Vertically check box to center the data between the top and bottom margins.

When you select the Show Margins button in the Print panel in the Backstage View (Ctrl+P) to modify the margin settings directly, you can also massage the column widths as well as the margins. To change one of the margins, position the mouse pointer on the desired margin marker (the pointer shape changes to a double-headed arrow) and drag the marker with your mouse in the appropriate direction. When you release the mouse button, Excel redraws the page, using the new margin setting. You may gain or lose columns or rows, depending on what kind of adjustment you make. Changing the column widths is the same story: Drag the column marker to the left or right to decrease or increase the width of a particular column.

Getting the lay of the landscape

The drop-down menu attached to the Orientation button in the Page Setup group of the Ribbon's Page Layout tab contains two options:

- ✔ **Portrait (the default):** Printing runs parallel to the short edge of the paper
- ✔ **Landscape:** Printing runs parallel to the long edge of the paper

Because many worksheets are far wider than they are tall (such as budgets or sales tables that track expenditures over 12 months), you may find that wider worksheets page better if you switch the orientation from Portrait mode (which accommodates fewer columns on a page because the printing runs parallel to the short edge of the page) to Landscape mode.

In Figure 5-5, you can see the Print Preview window with the first page of a report in Landscape mode. For this report, Excel can fit three more columns of information on this page in Landscape mode than it can in Portrait mode. However, because this page orientation accommodates fewer rows, the total page count for this report increases from two pages in Portrait mode to four pages in Landscape mode.

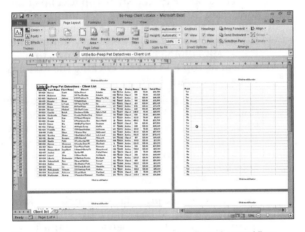

Figure 5-5: A Landscape mode report in Page Layout View.

Putting out the print titles

Excel's Print Titles feature enables you to print particular row and column headings on each page of the report. Print titles are important in multipage reports where the columns and rows of related data spill over to other pages that no longer show the row and column headings on the first page.

To designate rows and/or columns as the print titles for a report, follow these steps:

1. **Click the Print Titles button on the Page Layout tab on the Ribbon or press Alt+PI.**

   The Page Setup dialog box appears with Sheet tab selected (refer to Figure 5-6).

   To designate worksheet rows as print titles, go to Step 2a. To designate worksheet columns as print titles, go to Step 2b.

2a. **Select the Rows to Repeat at Top text box and then drag through the rows with information you want to appear at the top of each page in the worksheet below. If necessary, reduce the Page Setup dialog box to just the Rows to Repeat at Top text box by clicking the text box's Collapse/Expand button.**

   For the example shown in Figure 5-6, I clicked the Collapse/Expand button associated with the Rows to Repeat at Top text box and then dragged through rows 1 and 2 in column A of the Little Bo Peep Pet Detectives – Client List worksheet. Excel entered the row range $1:$2 in the Rows to Repeat at Top text box.

   Excel indicates the print-title rows in the worksheet by placing a dotted line (that moves like a marquee) on the border between the titles and the information in the body of the report.

2b. **Select the Columns to Repeat at Left text box and then drag through the range of columns with the information you want to appear at the left edge of each page of the printed report in the worksheet below. If necessary, reduce the Page Setup dialog box to just the Columns to Repeat at Left text box by clicking the text box's Collapse/Expand button.**

   Excel indicates the print-title columns in the worksheet by placing a dotted line (that moves like a marquee) on the border between the titles and the information in the body of the report.

3. **Click OK or press Enter to close the Page Setup dialog box.**

   The dotted line showing the border of the row and/or column titles disappears from the worksheet.

In Figure 5-6, rows 1 and 2 containing the worksheet title and column headings for the Little Bo Peep Pet Detectives client database are designated as the print titles for the report in the Page Setup dialog box. In Figure 5-7, you can see the Print Preview window with the second page of the report. Note how these print titles appear on all pages of the report.

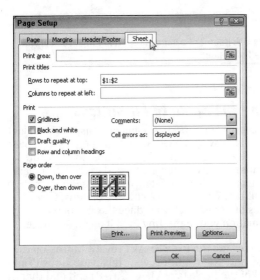

Figure 5-6: Specify the rows and columns to use as print titles on the Sheet tab of the Page Setup dialog box.

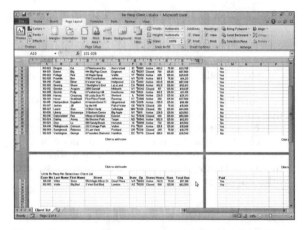

Figure 5-7: Page 2 of a sample report in Print Preview with defined print titles.

Using the Scale to Fit buttons

If your printer supports scaling options, you're in luck. You can always get a worksheet to fit on a single page simply by selecting the 1 Page option on the Width and Height drop-down menus attached to their command buttons in the Scale to Fit group on the Ribbon's Page Layout tab. When you select these options, Excel figures out how much to reduce the size of the information you're printing to fit it all on one page.

After clicking the Page Break Preview button on the Status bar, you might preview this page in the Print panel of the Backstage View (Ctrl+P) and find that the printing is just too small to read comfortably. Go back to the Normal worksheet view (Esc), select the Page Layout tab on the Ribbon, and try changing the number of pages in the Width and Height drop-down menus in the Scale to Fit group.

Instead of trying to stuff everything on one page, check out how your worksheet looks if you fit it on two pages across. Try this: Select 2 Pages on the Width button's drop-down menu on the Page Layout tab and leave 1 Page selected in the Height drop-down list button. Alternatively, see how the worksheet looks on two pages down: Select 1 Page on the Width button's drop-down menu and 2 Pages on the Height button's drop-down menu.

 After using the Width and Height Scale to Fit options, you may find that you don't want to scale the printing. Cancel scaling by selecting Automatic on both the Width and Height drop-down menus and then entering **100** in the Scale text box (or select 100% with its spinner buttons).

Using the Print buttons in the Sheet Options group

The Sheet Options group contains two very useful Print check boxes (neither of which is selected automatically). The first is in the Gridlines column, and the second is in the Headings column:

✓ Select the Print check box in the Gridlines column to print the column and row gridlines on each page of the report.

✓ Select the Print check box in the Headings column to print the row headings with the row numbers and the column headings with the column letters on each page of the report.

 Select both check boxes (by clicking them to put check marks in them) when you want the printed version of your spreadsheet data to closely match its onscreen appearance. This is useful when you need to use the cell references on the printout to help you later locate the cells in the actual worksheet that need editing.

From Header to Footer

Headers and footers are simply standard text that appears on every page of the report. A header prints in the top margin of the page, and a footer prints in the bottom margin. Both are centered vertically in the margins. Unless you specify otherwise, Excel does not automatically add either a header or footer to a new workbook.

Use headers and footers in a report to identify the document used to produce the report and display page numbers and the date and time of printing.

Add a header or footer to a report in Page Layout View. Switch to this view by clicking the Page Layout View button on the Status bar, by clicking the Page Layout View button on the Ribbon's View tab, or by pressing Alt+WP.

When the worksheet is in Page Layout View, position the mouse pointer over the section in the top margin of the first page marked Click to Add Header or in the bottom margin of the first page marked Click to Add Footer.

To create a centered header or footer, click the center section of this header/footer area to set the insertion point in the middle of the section. To add a left-aligned header or footer, click the left section to set the insertion point flush with the left edge. To add a right-aligned header or footer, click the right section to set the insertion point flush with the right edge.

Immediately after setting the insertion point in the left, center, or right section of the header/footer area, Excel adds a Header & Footer Tools contextual tab with its own Design tab (see Figure 5-8). The Design tab is divided into Header & Footer, Header & Footer Elements, Navigation, and Options groups.

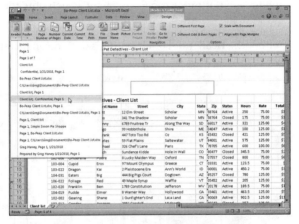

Figure 5-8: Defining a new header using the buttons on the Design tab of the Header & Footer Tools contextual tab.

Adding an auto header or footer

The Header and Footer command buttons on the Design tab of the Header & Footer Tools contextual tab enable you to add stock headers and footers in an instant. Simply click the appropriate command button and then click the header or footer example you want to use on the Header or Footer drop-down menu that appears.

To create the centered header and footer for the report shown in Figure 5-9, I selected Client List (name of worksheet), Confidential (stock text), and Page 1 (current page number) on the Header command button's drop-down menu.

To set up the footer, I chose Page 1 of ? in the Footer command button's drop-down menu, which puts the current page number with the total number of pages, in the report. You can select this paging option on either the Header or Footer button's drop-down menu.

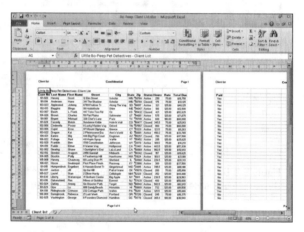

Figure 5-9: The first page of a report in Page Layout View shows you how the header and footer will print.

Check out the results in Figure 5-9, which is the first page of the report in Page Layout View. Here you can see the header and footer as they will print. You can

also see how choosing Page 1 of ? works in the footer:
On the first page, you see the centered footer *Page 1
of 4;* on the second page, the centered footer reads
Page 2 of 4.

 If, after selecting some stock header or footer
info, you decide that you no longer need either
the header or footer printed in your report, you
can remove it. Simply click the (None) option at
the top of the Header button's or Footer button's
drop-down menu. (Remember that the Design
tab with the Header and Footer command
buttons under the Header & Footer Tools
contextual tab is selected on the Ribbon the
moment you click the header or footer in Page
Layout View.)

Solving Page Break Problems

The Page Break preview feature in Excel enables you
to spot and fix page break problems in an instant,
such as when the program wants to split information
across different pages that you know should always
be on the same page.

Figure 5-10 shows a worksheet in Page Break Preview
with an example of a bad vertical page break that you
can remedy by adjusting the location of the page
break on Page 1 and Page 3. Given the page size,
orientation, and margin settings for this report, Excel
breaks the page between columns K and L. This break
separates the Paid column (L) from all the others in
the client list, effectively putting this information on
its own Page 3 and Page 4 (not shown in Figure 5-10).

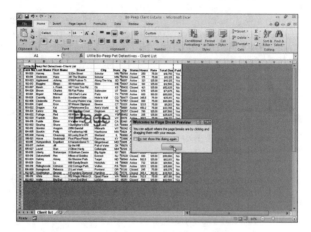

Figure 5-10: Preview page breaks in a report with Page Break Preview.

To prevent the data in the Paid column from printing on its own pages, you need to move the page break to a column on the left. In this case, I moved the page break to between columns G (with the zip code data) and H (containing the account status information) so that the name and address information stays together on Page 1 and Page 2 and the other client data is printed together on Page 3 and Page 4. Figure 5-11 shows vertical page breaks in the Page Break Preview worksheet view, which you can accomplish by following these steps:

1. **Click the Page Break Preview button (the third one in the cluster to the left of the Zoom slider) on the Status bar, or click View⇨Page Break Preview on the Ribbon or press Alt+WI.**

This takes you into a Page Break Preview worksheet view that shows your worksheet data at a
reduced magnification (60 percent of normal in
Figure 5-11) with the page numbers displayed in
large light type and the page breaks shown by
heavy lines between the columns and rows of the
worksheet.

The first time you choose this command, Excel
displays a Welcome to Page Break Preview dialog
box (refer to Figure 5-10). To prevent this dialog
box from reappearing each time you use Page
Break Preview, click the Do Not Show This Dialog
Again check box before you close the Welcome to
Page Break Preview alert dialog box.

2. **Click OK or press Enter to get rid of the
   Welcome to Page Break Preview alert dialog
   box.**

3. **Position the mouse pointer somewhere on the
   page break indicator (one of the heavy lines
   surrounding the representation of the page)
   that you need to adjust; when the pointer
   changes to a double-headed arrow, drag the
   page indicator to the desired column or row
   and release the mouse button.**

For the example shown in Figure 5-11, I dragged
the page break indicator between Page 1 and
Page 3 to the left so that it's between columns G
and H. Excel placed the page break at this point,
which puts all the name and address information
together on Page 1 and Page 2. This new page
break then causes all the other columns of client
data to print together on Page 3 and Page 4.

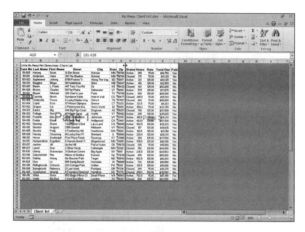

Figure 5-11: Page 1 of the report after adjusting the page breaks in the Page Break Preview worksheet view.

4. **After you finish adjusting the page breaks in Page Break Preview (and, presumably, printing the report), click the Normal button (the first one in the cluster to the left of the Zoom slider) on the Status bar, or click View⇨Normal on the Ribbon or press Alt+WL to return the worksheet to its regular view of the data.**

You can also insert your own manual page breaks at the cell cursor's position by clicking Insert Page Break on the Breaks button's drop-down menu on the Page Layout tab (Alt+PBI) and remove them by clicking Remove Page Break on this menu (Alt+PBR). To remove all manual page breaks that you've inserted into a report, click Reset All Page Breaks on the Breaks button's drop-down menu (Alt+PBA).

Letting Your Formulas All Hang Out

A basic printing technique you may need occasionally is printing the formulas in a worksheet instead of printing the calculated results of the formulas. You can check over a printout of the formulas in your worksheet to make sure you haven't done anything stupid (like replace a formula with a number or use the wrong cell references in a formula) before you distribute the worksheet companywide.

Before you can print a worksheet's formulas, you have to display the formulas, rather than their results, in the cells by clicking the Show Formulas button (the one with the icon that looks like a page of a calendar with a tiny 15 above an *fx*) in the Formula Auditing group on the Ribbon's Formulas tab (Alt+MH).

Excel then displays the contents of each cell in the worksheet the way they appear in the Formula bar or when you're editing them in the cell. Notice that value entries lose their number formatting, formulas appear in their cells (Excel widens the columns with best-fit so that the formulas appear in their entirety), and long text entries no longer spill into neighboring blank cells.

Excel allows you to toggle between the normal cell display and the formula cell display by pressing Ctrl+~. (That is, press Ctrl and the key with the tilde on top.) This key — usually found in the upper-left corner of your keyboard — does double-duty as a tilde and a weird backward accent mark. (Don't confuse that backward accent mark with the apostrophe that appears on a key below the quotation mark!)

After Excel displays the formulas in the worksheet, you are ready to print it as you would any other report. You can include the worksheet column letters and row numbers as headings in the printout so that if you do spot an error, you can pinpoint the cell reference right away.

 To include the row and column headings in the printout, put a check mark in the Print check box in the Headings column on the Sheet Options group of the Page Layout tab of the Ribbon before you send the report to the printer.

After you print the worksheet with the formulas, return the worksheet to normal by clicking the Show Formulas button on the Formulas tab of the Ribbon or by pressing Ctrl+~.

Chapter 6

Top Ten Beginner Basics

• •

*I*f these ten items are all you master in Excel 2010, you'll still be way ahead of the competition. When all is said and done, this top ten list lays out the fundamental skills required to use Excel 2010 successfully.

Starting Excel 2010

From the Windows 7 or Vista taskbar, click the Start button, type **exc** in the Search Programs and Files text box, and then with Microsoft Excel 2010 selected in the Programs section, press Enter.

Auto-Launching Excel 2010

To launch Excel 2010 automatically when you open an Excel workbook that needs editing (in the Documents window in Windows 7 and Vista), simply locate the folder containing the Excel workbook you want to edit and double-click its file icon.

Scrolling

To locate a part of a worksheet that you cannot see onscreen, click the scroll bars at the right and bottom of the workbook window to bring new parts of the worksheet into view.

Starting a New Workbook

To start a new workbook (containing three blank worksheets) using the Excel default template, simply press Ctrl+N. To open a new workbook based on another template, choose File➪New or press Alt+FN and then select the template to use in the New section of the Backstage View, where you can select a template or download one from Office.com. To add a new worksheet to a workbook (should you need more than three), click the Insert Worksheet button to the immediate right of the last tab at the bottom of the Worksheet area.

Activating an Open Workbook

To activate an open workbook and display it onscreen (in front of any others you have open), click the Ribbon's View tab, then click the window to activate in the Switch Windows button's drop-down menu (or press Alt+WW followed by the window's number). To locate a particular worksheet in the active workbook, click that worksheet's sheet tab at the bottom of the workbook document window. To display more sheet tabs, click the sheet scrolling arrows on the left side of the bottom of the workbook window.

Entering Stuff into a Worksheet

To enter stuff in a worksheet, select the cell where the information should appear; then begin typing. When you finish, click the Enter button on the Formula bar (the one with the check mark) or press Tab, Enter, or one of the arrow keys.

Editing Contents of a Cell

To edit the stuff you entered into a cell already, double-click the cell or position the cell pointer in the cell and press F2. Excel then positions the insertion point at the end of the cell entry and goes into Edit mode (see Chapter 2 for details). When you finish correcting the entry, click the Enter button on the Formula bar or press Tab or Enter.

Choosing Excel Commands

To choose one of the many Excel commands on the Ribbon, click the Ribbon tab, locate the group containing the command button, and then click the button. (Or, press the Alt key to display the hot keys on the Ribbon and then type the letter of the tab you want to select followed by the letter(s) of the command button to use.) To choose a command in Backstage View, choose File and then click its menu option or press Alt+F followed by the option's hot key letter. To choose a command on the Quick Access toolbar, click its command button.

Saving Your Work

To save a copy of your workbook to your hard drive the first time around, click the Save button on the Quick Access toolbar or press Ctrl+S. Next, designate the drive and folder directory where the file should be located, replace the temporary `Book1.xlsx` file-name in the File Name text box with your own file-name (up to 255 characters long, including spaces), and then click the Save button. To save a workbook so that older versions of Excel can open it, click the Save As option on the File tab and click the Excel 97-2003 Workbook (*.xls) option in the Save as Type drop-down menu.

Exiting Excel

To exit Excel when you're done working with the program, choose File⇨Exit or press Alt+F4 or Alt+FX. If the workbook you have open contains unsaved changes, Excel 2010 asks whether you want to save the workbook before closing Excel and returning to Windows. Before you shut off your computer, be sure to use the Shut Down command on the Start menu to shut down the Windows operating system.